How to Have a Wildly Successful Career in Compliance

LEARN THE SECRETS OF CAREER DEVELOPMENT AND
COLLABORATION TO BECOME AN IN-DEMAND
BUSINESS ASSET

Kristy Grant-Hart

Brentham House Publishing Company Ltd.
Covent Garden

HOW TO HAVE A WILDLY SUCCESSFUL CAREER IN COMPLIANCE

Brentham House Publishing Company
71-75 Shelton Street
Covent Garden
London, WC2H 9JQ
www.brenthamhousepublishing.com

Brentham House Publishing Company books may be purchased for educational, business or sales promotional use. For information, please email the Special Markets Department at Info@BrenthamHousePublishing.com.

FIRST EDITION
A CIP Record of this book is available from the British Library.

ISBN: 978-0-9934788-7-1 (soft cover edition)
ISBN: 978-0-9934788-8-8 (electronic edition)

Brentham House
Publishing Company Ltd.
COVENT GARDEN

"Kristy Grant-Hart captures the wisdom, philosophy, and business savvy of multi-industry compliance officers. She provides comprehensive guidance on myriad topics including business value, personal branding and salary negotiation. These are essential components to professional development at varying levels of a compliance career. This is my new go-to resource for achieving a Wildly Successful Career in Compliance, and it should be for all compliance professionals."

- *Walter E. Johnson,*
Director of Compliance and Ethics at Kforce Government Solutions, Inc.

"At last! After years of reading dry, academic Compliance books, I finally have a practical, entertaining and wise guidebook that will help me become a more efficient and engaged compliance officer. Excellent.""

- *Patrick O'Kane*
Data Protection Officer and author of GDPR: Fix it Fast! Apply GDPR to Your Company in 10 Simple Steps

Contents

For my mother, Kathy Elwood – the best cheerleader the world has ever known, fearless warrior in the face of challenge, and the inspiration behind my every achievement.

Introduction

"Long ago, I realized that success leaves clues, and that people who produce outstanding results do specific things to create those results."
- Tony Robbins

Success leaves clues. Unexamined, it may seem that everyone's compliance story is different, or that success is a matter of luck. Sure, some things will always make a difference, like hard work or kissing up to the boss. But other things may not be so obvious, like knowing the options available to you within the profession so you can strategically plan your next move, or knowing how to negotiate a job offer to maximize not only your salary, but your ability to rise quickly to the next level.

This book is for seekers – those who want to create not just a job in the compliance field, but a Wildly Successful career. It is meant just as much for the person just starting in compliance, as for the seasoned Chief Compliance and Ethics Officer. The compliance field is rife with opportunity, and those who are properly prepared are in the best position to outrun the competition and achieve great results.

Compliance and ethics jobs are growing as never before. Often when I deliver speeches, I ask the audience how many of them grew up wanting to be a compliance officer. Laughter is usually the answer to that question. After all, compliance wasn't a profession or a career choice 20, 30 or 40 years ago. That's changing.

Colleges and law schools are increasingly offering classes and degrees in compliance. Certification programs like the CCEP (Certified Compliance and Ethics Professional) are separating out the trained from the not-yet-there. And while many people in the early days were simply assigned to compliance without knowing what it was, many now are actively seeking out the role.

I'm deeply passionate about the role the compliance profession is playing in the world. Compliance officers are literally changing the way business gets done. Where bribery used to be commonplace and seen as a cost of doing business, now compliance teams implement programs to stop it before it starts. Where money laundering was seen as something inevitable, now know-your-customer laws require compliance officers to verify customer identities at all major banks in the world. And where terrorist funding used to sneak below the radar, now trade sanctions stop business from moving money to groups intent on murder and destruction.

> *Compliance officers are literally changing the way business gets done.*

Compliance officers play an intricate and critical role in the shift toward more ethical business practices. Ours is a proud profession. It is sometimes lonely, but at the end of the day, we're ensuring business is done properly and with transparency. Ours is a mission, or a calling, and I want everyone in compliance to succeed like never before.

This book isn't just for compliance officers. It's for everyone in the compliance profession – managers, investigators, anti-money laundering officers, policy writers, HR folks with some compliance obligations, corporate ethicists, jurists, lawyers, accountants – in short, anyone who works in compliance or wants to work in compliance. I use the words "compliance officer" throughout this book as shorthand for anyone working in the profession, but fear not! If you work in compliance, this book is for you.

Crowd-Sourcing the Information

This book contains the wisdom I have acquired in my fifteen years of practicing in the compliance profession – first in private legal practice, then in-house as a Director and Chief Compliance Officer (CCO), then as the owner of a multi-national compliance consulting company.

I've created compliance programs from the ground up. I've performed compliance training in forty-three countries on five continents. I've been a professor of Global Compliance and Ethics at Delaware Law School, Widener University. I've written two books (*How to Be a Wildly Effective Compliance Officer* and the *Wildly Strategic Compliance Officer's Workbook*) and countless blogs about the compliance profession. Along the way, I've been shortlisted for awards, and brought in to do keynote speeches before thousands of compliance professionals.

Which means, as usual, I have a lot to say! But as I was writing this book, I quickly realized I didn't have the answers to all the questions. For instance, I've never worked in-house in financial services or healthcare. I've never been part of the government or a recruiter operating in the compliance field. How would I credibly talk about such things?

The answers came from generous members of the compliance profession. I interviewed innumerable people about their careers and obtained written answers to questionnaires from others. I read reports on the state of the profession and created a survey that ran via LinkedIn and through my website that helped me obtain critical insights into how various areas of the profession operate. All of this is to say, this isn't really my book – it's a collection of information passed through me, representing the experiences of thousands within the compliance profession.

What's Inside

This book is meant to help you become a Wildly Successful Compliance Officer. We start with the fundamental question – do you really want to be in compliance? We've got a quiz to help you see if this profession is right for you. Next, we'll reveal how to showcase your relevant qualifications on your CV/resume (even if you don't think you have any).

After that, we'll do a deep dive into the six-fold path. We'll take a look at the pros and cons of accepting an in-house role in financial services, healthcare, and general corporate compliance. We'll get advice from people who've been in each – about what to do to get into the profession and how to be successful once you're there. Next, we'll look at alternatives to in-house compliance, such as government work, consulting, and working for compliance-related vendors. This section is meant to stimulate you to plan your next move, and to help you plan your long-term career.

Once you've decided where you'd like to go next, we'll strategically run through whether you should take a particular job that's offered to you. If the answer is yes, the next section will help you to negotiate the very best deal possible. There's even a special section addressing women's unique challenges in negotiating for what we're worth.

Next, we'll talk about how to move up the ladder (or jungle gym). We'll learn the importance of understanding the business and knowing the numbers, and about how to secure a fantastic mentor or champion.

Once you've done your strategic planning, we'll jump into raising your profile. Speaking, writing, getting on podcasts and in the press – we'll cover it all. We'll deal with what's stopping you from raising your profile, and get into specific techniques for overcoming fear and dealing with criticism.

Next, we'll talk about how and why you should join compliance-related organizations, and how to create your personal compliance-related brand.

We'll then get into the crucial details of collaboration. We'll do a deep-dive into specific ways of working with the Human Resources, Legal, Internal Audit and Procurement departments. We'll work through the best uses of trade associations, conferences, outside counsel, consulting firms, technology vendors, and recruiters.

Last, we'll take a peek into the future of the compliance profession, so that you can be prepared to be even more Wildly Successful in the future.

Success Leaves Clues

In this book are the secrets of career development and collaboration that will help you succeed at higher levels than you ever have before. Taken together, this book will provide a roadmap to help you to get from where you are now to heights you may not have imagined possible. It is my fervent belief that the work you are doing as a compliance officer is changing the world. The better you are at building your career, the more the compliance profession – and therefore the world – will benefit. Are you ready? Let's go!

Chapter 1: First Things First -- Is a Career in Compliance Right for You?

Before we dive into how to build a Wildly Successful career in compliance, let's take a step back and find out if a career in compliance is right for you. After all, while I love the work I do, I recognize compliance isn't for everyone. If compliance is a bad fit for you, it's best to know that up front to save yourself changing careers in short order.

One of the fascinating things about compliance is that it tends to draw people from many fields. Auditors and lawyers are the most likely candidates for compliance jobs, but I've seen people from operations, accounting, management and administration come into compliance as well. Heck, I have an undergraduate degree in film and television, so if I can end up in compliance (loving it), then anyone can!

Compliance requires a specific skill set and set of interests. The more of these qualities you have, the more likely you are to enjoy a career in compliance.

Quiz: Is Compliance the Right Career for You?

Diana Trevley, my Los Angeles-based business partner in Spark Compliance Consulting, wrote this quiz to help people determine whether they would enjoy a career in compliance.

In order to assess whether compliance is for you, give yourself one point for each of the following statements that applies to you:

1._ I am able to travel out of town on a semi-regular basis without it disrupting my personal life and obligations.

2._ I have an interest in learning about different cultures and I am willing to respect cultural differences.

3._ When faced with delivering difficult news or taking a stand I know others don't agree with, I am able to be diplomatic and non-confrontational without acquiescing to the pressure to be silent or agree with the majority opinion.

4._ When I think something is not right. either legally or ethically, I am able to speak my mind, even if I know that others do not agree.

5._ I am comfortable with public speaking in both large and small groups.

6._ I enjoy spending much of my day in front of a computer.

7._ I am able to handle a variety of tasks and projects without getting overwhelmed or missing deadlines.

8._ I think it is more important to do what is right than to make other people feel comfortable.

9.__ It is acceptable for me to have a career where I some-times have to work late into the night, on weekends, or on holidays.

10.__ I like learning new things.

11.__ I consider myself a person of high ethical character. For example, I do not lie on my resume, and I don't steal from my employer.

12.__ I consider myself a good listener. When someone is speaking, I listen to what they have to say and consider it, ra-ther than waiting for my turn to speak.

13.__ I ponder the root cause of a problem.

14.__ I try to respond to my emails as soon as possible. I do not like a messy inbox.

15.__ I find it relatively easy to stay relaxed and focused, even when there is pressure regarding a deadline or an outcome.

16.__ I find that I am able to be impartial and consider the facts when assessing a situation, putting my personal feelings aside.

17.__ I value justice more than mercy.

18.__ I am organized and enjoy putting things in order.

19.__ I like to be engaged in a fast-paced and active job.

20.__ I believe in following the rules, even if the outcome is not what others or I would prefer.

21.__ I tend to be specific and literal when talking to people.

22.__ I like to think of new and creative ways to solve problems.

23.__ Technology doesn't scare me.

24.__ I consider myself to be highly motivated and energetic.

25.__ I have no difficulties coming up with a personal timetable and sticking to it.

26.__ I adapt well to new and unexpected situations.

27.__ I think it is important to establish a process and do things the same way each time.

28.__ I keep a calm head in a crisis and am able to act rationally, even when others around me are upset.

29.__ I do not feel the need to be the most popular person in the room.

30.__ I trust facts, concrete examples and proof, rather than relying solely on my intuition or gut instincts.

31.__ I think first, then act, rather than rushing to take action before I have considered my options.

32.__ Group discussions stimulate me and give me energy.

33.__ I enjoy finding more efficient ways to do things.

34.__ I keep confidential information confidential, and I do not gossip at work.

35.__ I am not intimidated by people in powerful positions, such as CEOs of companies or high-level government officials.

36.__ I am comfortable working in a profession where the right course of action is not always clear.

37.__ I want to make the world a better place.

38.__ I believe it is not only important for a business to make money, but to be socially responsible and try to improve the lives of its employees and customers.

39.__ People have told me that I am very persuasive.

40.__ I am a team player.

41.__ I don't feel a strong need for recognition for everything that I do.

42.__ I find it easy to introduce myself to other people and to be sociable.

43.__ I think it is important to develop good relationships with people at work, even if I don't work directly for them or with them.

44.__ I am able to control my emotions and think rationally during high-stress situations.

45.__ I consider myself to be a natural leader.

46.__ If I don't know something, I will take the time to learn it until I am an expert on the subject.

47.__ I am able to work independently on projects.

48.__ Others have told me I have good judgment and rely on me for advice.

49.__ I can take complex subject matter and make it comprehensible to a layperson.

50.__ I enjoy talking with the workers and not just the executives.

51. The following careers sound like fun to me:

- __ Investigator
- __ Middle School Teacher
- __ Policy Writer
- __ Diplomat
- __ International Speaker
- __ Police Officer
- __ Project Manager
- __ Auditor
- __ Salesperson

Total up your score here: ___

Scoring

If you scored less than 25, a career in corporate compliance may not be a good fit for you. If you scored between 26 and 40, corporate compliance may be a good choice for you, particularly if you consider specializing in a compliance role that best suits you and your goals. If you scored 41 or more, welcome to the profession! You'll love it here.

Rapid Movement

Now that you're sure you want to build a career in compliance, let's take some steps to make it Wildly Successful. There are many secrets to rapidly advancing your career. If you're going to have a career anyway, why not make it the best, most highly paid, celebrated career it can be?

My career in compliance advanced quickly. I'm certain that implementing the techniques I present in this book facilitated my quick ascent from lawyer to leading compliance professional.

Planning to succeed is the best way to make it happen. By committing to your career growth and deciding to take action, you'll move up through the compliance ranks at a much faster rate. If you're happy in your present position, following the steps and suggestions in this book will help you to give back to the profession, and inspire the younger compliance officers following in your footsteps. It will also help you to be in the best possible professional position if anything happens to your role, or if your company downsizes or goes out of business.

Planning to succeed is the best way to make it happen.

Careers are never static, even when they appear to be. Corporate mandates change, regulations shift, technology makes some sectors hot and others obsolete. By acting to keep your skills current, your network strong and your profile up-to-date, you'll provide yourself with the best insurance to ensure a smooth transition to another role or a promotion.

You don't have to take every piece of advice in this book in order to secure a bright future. If you were to take on everything in this book at once, you might not have time for your day job! However, small actions taken with consistency over time lead to big results. A monthly commitment to one or more of the techniques in this book will lead you to the best position possible for you within the profession.

Getting the Gig

Whether you're going for your first role in compliance, or your fifteenth, you'll always need a killer resume to get the job. Let's find out how to highlight the compliance-related qualifications on your CV or resume (even if you don't think you have any yet).

Chapter 2: The Compliance CV: How to Effectively Showcase Your Relevant Qualifications (Even if You Don't Think You Have Any)

I get an email almost daily from someone interested in getting into compliance, but they don't know where to start. If you're new to the profession (or trying to break in), you may not feel like you have enough qualifications to help your resume to stand out. However, you probably have more compliance-related skills than you think, and highlighting them is critical to joining the profession and moving up once you're in.

My business partner, Diana Trevley, successfully moved from litigation into compliance. She wrote the following section to help you to get where you want to go – fast.

There is No One Route

There is no one route to becoming a compliance professional. Some compliance professionals join the compliance department after working for years at their company. Others are lawyers who have worked in law firms or for the Department of Justice. Some are accountants or investigators, and others have worked within a regulatory agency. This diversity within a company's compliance department helps to foster innovative ideas and avoid the "group think" that might occur in a department composed of individuals with the same educational background and work experience. It also means the field is relatively wide open for those who decide they too want to become compliance professionals.

> *There is no one route to becoming a compliance professional.*

As compliance and ethics becomes a more established profession, managers often prefer to hire someone with prior experience, rather than take a chance on someone new. This is why it is so important for those wishing to pursue long-term careers in compliance to create a CV that showcases how their education, job experience, and skills will be valuable to a compliance and ethics department.

List Advanced Degrees and/or Compliance-Related Certifications Immediately After Your Name on Your CV

If you have any advanced degrees and compliance-related certifications, list them immediately after your name on the top of your CV. For example, if you have an MBA, the top of your CV should read "Jane Smith, MBA." Not all compliance professionals have advanced degrees or certifications, and you want potential employers to see right away—without having to search through the text of your CV—that you have these additional qualifications.

If you don't have a compliance-related certification, such as the Certified Compliance and Ethics Professional (CCEP) designation, consider whether your past work experience and education qualifies you to obtain such certification, and whether it would be a good investment of your time for you to pursue one.

If You Are Brand New to Compliance, Add a Brief "Objective" Section at the Top of Your CV

When I decided to pursue a career in corporate compliance, a Chief Compliance Officer suggested I add an "Objective" heading at the top of my CV and provide one to three sentences summing up my career goals.

At first, I was reluctant to add such a section, because I had never seen one on a professional CV; it seemed amateur. I thought my career objectives should be in my cover letter.

The Chief Compliance Officer mentioned two facts that changed my mind. First, he said many hiring managers rarely read job applicants' cover letters. Second, he said unless I made it immediately clear on my CV that I was actively pursuing a new career path in compliance, it might look, based on my past work history as a litigator, that I was just aimlessly sending out my CV to any job opening without any real interest in compliance.

Include Your Interest in Compliance in Your Cover Letter

While your cover letter may go unread, include one when you apply for a position, as it is still standard practice. Be sure to highlight all the vital information contained in your CV and state clearly why you are interested in a career in compliance and ethics.

Gather 10 Corporate Compliance Job Postings, and Circle the Skills and/or Experience You Already Have

When you review compliance-related job postings, you will notice a clear pattern of what hiring managers are looking for, such as knowledge of the Federal Sentencing Guidelines, anti-bribery legislation, or excellent communication skills. Your CV should reflect these qualifications to the extent possible.

When describing your prior positions, emphasize the work you did that is relevant to tasks you will be doing as a compliance officer. This will allow hiring managers to see how your unique skill set will be useful within the compliance department. Professionals with legal, accounting, investigatory or human resource experience have valuable skills they should be sure to emphasize.

Lawyers should emphasize their analytical, writing, and investigative skills. Those who have worked in human resources should focus on how they've dealt with internal complaints and adhering to company policies. Those who have worked in accounting will want to highlight their auditing and analytical skills.

Consider Whether Your Prior Work Experience Allows You to List Any of These Qualifications on Your CV:

- Working with laws and regulations
- Working within a highly regulated industry
- Working at a large, multinational company
- Working within the specific industry in which you want to work
- Managing projects, particularly large projects, or those that entail working across different departments
- Creating documents that govern company policies or standard operating procedures
- Acting as the face of the company

- Working with outside vendors
- Handling complaints at the company – both internal and external
- Leading or taking part in investigations
- Conducting due diligence on new hires or other companies
- Creating and/or conducting training
- Writing legal, financial, or other complex documents
- Creating and/or delivering presentations to high-level executives
- Reviewing internal financial records and working in the audit department
- Ensuring proper documentation is in place for the company's actions
- Conducting risk assessments, even in an informal context
- Working in sales or another position that requires people skills and the ability to persuade others
- Taking corrective or remedial action at the company when things go wrong
- Interacting with government officials, even on a local level
- Handling marketing and publicity efforts, such as creating posters, flyers, or sending out email notices to highlight the company's actions
- Traveling for work, particularly internationally

Include a "Qualifications" Section that Highlights Your "Soft" Skills

"Soft skills," such as excellent communication and the capacity to build consensus, are vital for compliance professionals. Listing your soft skills on your CV is important because it shows hiring managers not only that you have these skills, but also you recognize they are important for the job. As noted previously, combing through compliance and ethics job postings is a good way to get an idea of what type of skills you may want to list.

Limit Your CV to Two Pages

Distill your experience, education, and qualifications down to two pages, unless you have been working in compliance for more than a few years. It is common knowledge that hiring managers frequently look at each CV for less than a minute.

People are more inclined to read short documents when they are very busy. Committing to a concise CV forces you to only include information directly relevant to compliance, rather than a laundry list of your achievements over the years. No one (with the possible exception of your parents) has the time or inclination to read about every duty you had at your last job, or every club you joined while at university.

While it is important to include your work history when describing your previous jobs, do so in a way that emphasizes the qualifications you have that directly relate to the job for which you're applying.

People are more inclined to read short documents when they are very busy.

Create One Master CV That Accurately Reflects Your Qualifications

Many headhunters suggest you tailor each CV you send out to match the desired qualifications and industry of each job posting. To make this easier, create one master CV that accurately reflects what you will bring to the table as a compliance and ethics professional. Then, you can add minor tweaks as needed, depending on the job posting. For example, if the role requires training employees, you can add information to emphasize your public speaking experience.

Include Hyperlinks in Your CV

Include hyperlinks to your LinkedIn profile and to publications you have written that can be accessed online. Put the hyperlink directly into the text: for example, someone should be able to click on the title of your publication in order to access the article. Adding hyperlinks directly into your CV allows hiring managers to quickly access more information about you if they want to learn more without weighing them down with additional documents.

Once Your CV is Nearing Completion, Ask Several Compliance Professionals to Look It Over and Get Their Thoughts

Ask compliance professionals you know to look at your near-finished CV. They may have valuable suggestions as to what additional information you should include, or what you might consider omitting, to best showcase your qualifications.

Keep in mind everyone will have a different opinion, and it will be impossible to incorporate all suggestions into the final product, so ultimately you need to rely on your own judgment. Also, don't send your friends and mentors a CV that hasn't been thoroughly proofread. Your friends are there to provide suggestions on the content, not comb through the document for errors.

Do Not Lie or Exaggerate on Your CV!

This should be a given, but there are many people who send out CVs that don't accurately reflect their experience or education. As a compliance and ethics professional, you are expected to adhere to the highest standards of ethics and integrity. This should extend to your search for a job in compliance and ethics. Make sure you can back up everything you list on your CV, from the job descriptions to the dates that you worked, to your GPA at university.

Don't give up if your CV doesn't yield the responses you expected immediately. Network with other compliance professionals. Do what you can to gain experience or education in compliance while you search for a new position. Continue to send out your CV. Soon, you will find the perfect job for you.

And Now, to the Perfect Job!

And what is that perfect job? Ah – let's look at the options, shall we?

Chapter 3: Pathways to Success: Oh, the Places You'll Go!

"Cat: Where are you going?
Alice: Which way should I go?
Cat: That depends on where you are going.
Alice: I don't know.
Cat: Then it doesn't matter which way you go."
– Lewis Carol, Alice in Wonderland

Where will your career in compliance take you? Will you reach the Chief Compliance Officer role at the highest echelons of a public corporation? Will you ensure that government actors perform their roles at the highest levels of integrity? Or will you join an outside vendor in order to serve the compliance community?

There are many pathways to successful compliance-related careers. I've been down three of them.

My Winding Career Progression

My first full-time job was at Paramount Pictures, working for a vice president of film development. I worked in Hollywood for a number of years and then decided to go to law school. I went to law school because I wanted to travel. I had visions of being paid to travel while working on cases, and I couldn't wait to start. I went to school at night, working full time during the day as a legal secretary.

Law Firm Life

When I graduated, I took a job at Gibson, Dunn & Crutcher in Los Angeles. Since I wanted to work internationally, I looked around and realized some of the partners were working on really interesting anti-bribery cases and corporate monitorships. I made friends with the partners on these cases, and was staffed on several corporate monitorships, including that of Siemens, which at the time had the largest bribery-related fine in history.

Three years into my legal career, the opportunity to move to London for the LIBOR investigation came up. I embraced it eagerly. While in London, I met and then married my husband, Jonathan.

Since I was newly married and no longer wanted to move from London back to Los Angeles, I looked carefully at my skills and experiences, and then met with a recruiter in London. He said I should consider "compliance," a new field that required many of the practice areas I had developed. These included anti-bribery work, anti-trust/competition work and data privacy. I decided to go for it.

Welcome to Compliance

I left Gibson Dunn to work as the Director of Compliance for Europe, the Middle East and Africa for Carlson Wagonlit Travel. I'd never held an in-house role, but I'd worked closely with in-house teams during compliance-related corporate monitorships. My very first day, the president of the region shook my hand and said, "Welcome, Kristy. I have no idea what compliance is or what you'll do all day, but I hope you'll enjoy yourself here." There was much work to be done.

Sometime later, I was contacted via LinkedIn by a recruiter who worked for NBCUniversal. She'd seen my online profile and sent an email saying, "We can't find anyone with a compliance background and a film degree/experience except you." I was invited to apply for the Chief Compliance Officer role at United International Pictures, the joint distribution company for Paramount Pictures and Universal Pictures in 65+ countries. Several interviews later, I accepted the challenge. I loved my role as Chief Compliance Officer. Creating their program from scratch was a highlight of my career.

Book Publishing and Compliance Consulting

I founded Spark Compliance Consulting in February 2016, the same month *How to Be a Wildly Effective Compliance Officer* was published. Spark Compliance Consulting quickly expanded from London into the United States, and we have been performing work in the anti-bribery, anti-slavery, data privacy and ISO 37001 anti-bribery certification areas ever since.

The reason I share all of this is to say, I've been there. I've been in private practice in a global law firm; I've been in subordinate roles in compliance at corporations, as well as the Chief Compliance Officer. I've owned my own solopreneur firm that grew to become a global corporation. Each role has its own challenges and rewards. Which role is right for you? Let's discuss the options.

Pathways

The best path for you depends upon your skills, strengths, interests, and goals. Let's explore six different paths: (1) in-house corporate compliance (including financial services compliance, healthcare compliance and general corporate compliance), (2) in-house legal / business, (3) consulting/private practice, (4) government, (5) nonprofit/NGO, and (6) compliance-related vendor.

In-house Compliance Roles

Corporate compliance officers create and monitor processes and procedures that assist the employees of the company to behave ethically and in compliance with the law. Corporate compliance structures range from a single compliance professional to complex global groups, including hundreds of compliance professionals throughout the world.

People who thrive in corporate compliance tend to love the challenge of being deeply embedded in the business. They like to partner with the business, understand the direction the business is going, and work to make processes and procedures manageable in order for the company to be profitable. Many people move from one company to another as part of their career progression. Corporate compliance jobs offer relative stability, with a consistent paycheck and more predictable hours than private practice or consulting.

The downside to these roles is that they can become monotonous. Many people find once a compliance program is established, the day-to-day management of issues is less interesting. Other people find the constant requests from the business and firefighting to be hard to manage while maintaining a personal life.

Survey Says...

As I haven't worked in every area of compliance, I commissioned a wide-ranging survey of compliance officers across the profession to learn what they thought of their jobs. Financial services work can be quite different than healthcare compliance and general corporate compliance, and because of that, I asked each group what they thought of their jobs. What is the best thing about their area of compliance? What's the worst thing? And what advice would they give to someone who wants to join their specialty?

Financial Services Compliance

Financial services compliance officers primarily focus on industry-specific laws, as well as anti-money laundering and anti-bribery. They tend to have a specific remit, whether that is investment banking, insurance, securities, or consumer banking.

The Best Things About Working in Financial Services Compliance

Let's start with a fact: financial services compliance professionals tend to be the best paid. And while this is definitely a perk, people in financial services find much to laud about the area besides the big paychecks.

Chad Eslinger, Chief Compliance Officer, Insurance and Annuity at Voya Financial, said the best thing about financial services compliance is, "The thrill of supporting the customer experience!" He said he loves handling the investigations that ensure customer complaints are fully vetted and responded to properly. "I love working for our customers!"

Other compliance officers in financial services appreciate having "high-level oversight, with a plethora of possibilities."

Financial services regulations change quickly. James, a Senior Compliance and Financial Crime Manager, said he most enjoys the amount of regulatory change, which makes for "a very challenging and varied workload." Wawanesa Mutual Insurance Company's Compliance Manager, Sarah, said she most enjoys learning something new every day.

The Worst Things About Working in Financial Services Compliance

One common worry among financial service compliance officers is the threat of being held personally liable. Financial service regulators have begun prosecuting and fining compliance officers for corporate compliance failures, making the job a higher-risk undertaking than general corporate or healthcare compliance.

With greater regulation than other industries, financial services can be difficult. One compliance officer bemoaned that the worst thing about working in financial services compliance is, "Regulatory bureaucracy! The grind of the red tape to get things done can get old, but is generally a necessary evil." Another said that the lack of clarity from regulators was infuriating.

Of course, as with other areas of compliance, in financial services it is easy to be perceived as the bad guy.

Advice on Getting Into Financial Services Compliance

Because regulation changes so quickly in financial services, Jane Riley, Chief Compliance Officer at The Leaders Group, advises to "Be a generalist, and be interested in learning everything. What you study isn't nearly as important as being open to learning."

Several people noted that working in various parts of the business is helpful. One professional said, "I've worked in just about every job – consumer compliance, sales, production, vender management, etc. So what has worked well for me is that I have the perspective of what each business line employee faces each day. I can relate to the employee and their role in the organization." Another suggested to "work with various banking products, [to] gain understanding of the markets and services offered."

And last, passion is always important. "Be passionate about everything you do. Work harder than everyone around you, and good things will happen," said CCO Chad Eslinger.

Healthcare Compliance

Healthcare compliance is a large and growing sector of the compliance field. Like financial services, healthcare compliance can be highly specialized. Regulations abound, and regular government inspections mean healthcare compliance professionals are in high demand. Knowledge of privacy laws, such as the U.S. Health Insurance Portability and Accountability Act (HIPAA), and the European General Data Protection Regulation (GDPR), are especially critical in this field.

The Best Things About Working in Healthcare Compliance

Healthcare compliance can be especially rewarding because it benefits patients in a direct way. Regarding this patient focus, V. Duarte of Dignity Health said the satisfaction is in "knowing that my work will ultimately impact patient care … At the end of the day, it is about doing the right thing for the patients."

Healthcare professionals also thrive because of the variety in their work. Compliance specialist Rachel Kauffman said she is "always learning new and challenging things." Another healthcare specialist said she loves, "working with everyone in all areas of the company. You never know what to expect on any given day, and no two days are the same!"

The Worst Things About Working in Healthcare Compliance

"It can be very stressful and trying at times, especially when dealing with high-level executives and physicians. It can be a mentally draining job." Healthcare compliance comes with the special challenge of working with physicians and medical professionals. One compliance officer told me the doctors in her firm simply don't allocate time for compliance. They think it is for "less important people than themselves."

One compliance officer wrote that he hated the "lack of full leadership buy-in, the inaccessibility to the board, and insufficient resources," followed by, "Don't use my name on this one!" Another one said she felt frustrated by being brought into the business too late to add value.

Advice on Getting Into Healthcare Compliance

Several people noted the advantages of working in the healthcare field prior to joining healthcare compliance. One compliance professional said, "You need a good background in the healthcare field first, and then perhaps some education in business management or paralegal skills." Another noted, "It's great if people have had some type of operational experience in healthcare, to be able to understand basic terminology and know the type of work that you will help support in Compliance."

Healthcare compliance-related organizations can be of use. "The HCCA [Health Care Compliance Association] is a great resource ... You can connect with and initiate relationships with CCOs," said a current CCO. Rachel Kaufman said, "Go to the conferences and talk to the people that are doing what you do, and don't be afraid of what is around the corner."

What if you've never worked in healthcare compliance but already work in healthcare? Carrie, a senior compliance manager at a major pharmaceutical and medical device company provided this advice, "Become very familiar with the AdvaMed and PhRMA codes. Build your relationship with the Compliance Officer; be someone they can count on. If you are a manager, share with other managers how you partner with the compliance team and the efforts you are taking to advance the culture of compliance with your team."

She went on to say, "If your company supports it, try to work on a project or assignment with your compliance team. This will deepen your understanding into what they do and what the expectations are for the business-facing partners."

General Corporate Compliance

General corporate compliance involves any industry that is not highly regulated. From travel to entertainment to retail, corporate compliance and ethics is the broad-based name for compliance that doesn't follow a strict regulatory regime. Corporate compliance officers handle a great variety of areas, depending on the role and type of company. Some common areas for these professionals to manage include:

- Anti-bribery and Anti-corruption
- Anti-trust/Competition
- Conflicts of Interest
- Trade Sanctions

- Import/Export
- Data Privacy and Protection
- Policies and Procedures
- Training
- Harassment
- Corporate Ethics
- Anti-money Laundering
- Health and Safety
- Modern Slavery/Human Trafficking

The Best Things About Working in General Corporate Compliance

Most of my work (both in-house and in consulting) has been in general corporate compliance. The thing I love most about it is the opportunity to affect the business in a powerful way by creating and implementing processes that stop wrongdoing. Laura Ellis of Cisco Systems agrees with me. She says the thing she likes best about working in general corporate compliance is, "the vertical application of ethics and compliance across all areas of the business. The focus [is] on doing the right thing, not just for regulatory reasons, but to support the business as a whole."

One person enjoyed, "Not being regulated [so I'm] able to find the right program for my company's challenges."

The ability to work with many different facets of the business came up again and again. "The wide variety of things that you need to master to be effective, and the variety of things you deal with every day," were the best things about corporate compliance for one practitioner, while another said they enjoyed, "interacting with so many diverse groups of people and touching so many different parts of the company." Compliance Officer Darcy Southwell said, "I appreciate and enjoy working with (and learning from) all of our business units as we work to embed corporate compliance and ethics into every business unit."

The Worst Things About Working in General Corporate Compliance

"It's incredibly frustrating when the focus on growth, or revenue, or getting things done quickly conflicts with compliance and ethics strategies. It's often because an individual or team doesn't see the benefits of compliance and ethics, but it's still frustrating," said one corporate compliance officer. The focus on revenue and business growth can sometimes outweigh the commitment to compliance within a not-highly-regulated organization. "Sometimes you are left feeling as if you are all alone on an issue if senior leadership doesn't fully support you," said a CCO.

While not being highly regulated feels like a benefit to some compliance officers, others find themselves frustrated by the lack of regulatory heft behind their programs. A compliance manager told me, "Compliance is not as prominent as in healthcare or finance, so we're still working to build an industry framework. Much of compliance is still run by Legal." Another agreed, stating, "Not being regulated means having to go many rounds trying to convince management of the need for protection."

Advice on Getting into General Corporate Compliance

A big piece of advice for getting into general corporate compliance is to develop soft skills as well as learning regulation. One Senior Compliance Director advised to, "Master hard and soft skills equally. The hard skills get you started down a compliance path, but it is the soft skills that get you to a higher level of responsibility and success."

People also highlighted focusing on an industry you enjoy, and then finding compliance roles related to it. Such was the case with Joe Lloyd III, Tyson Food's Vice President, Ethics and Compliance Officer. Joe said, "Pick a field of study where your interests and passions are off the charts, and then focus on the compliance element(s) found within - they're always there. Microbiology was mine, which led me to food safety law, which led me to Tyson."

Certification is seen as a particularly important element to growing a corporate compliance career. "CISA/CISSP helps," said Tanuja Brundavan, Head - Risk, Audit, Compliance & Governance, IDM India, at Atos. Another compliance professional said, "The most valuable qualification I have is the CCEP-I. Whilst I have yet to need this on my CV, the course content has been invaluable."

Many people mentioned the value of group learning and education. A Senior Director of Corporation Compliance stated, "Attend training and compliance education events or an SCCE Compliance & Ethics Academy." Laura Ellis of Cisco commented, "My biggest piece of advice for meeting the right people is to attend conferences. Read LinkedIn articles and books, then approach the author/speaker. Explain your passion and ask to understand more."

Other Pathways

In-house corporate compliance isn't the only way to work within the broader compliance profession. You can also try being in-house counsel / General Counsel, a business leader, a consultant or lawyer in private practice, a worker in government compliance, non-governmental organizational compliance, or work for a vendor selling solutions to the compliance profession. Let's take a look at each.

In-house Counsel, Business Leader or General Counsel

Many people in the compliance field transition into or out of in-house counsel, general counsel or a business role. At some companies, future leaders are put through a rotation in the compliance department so they understand the risks and challenges facing the company from a compliance perspective.

Compliance professionals who move into in-house counsel or general counsel roles tend to enjoy contracts and the legal part of the profession. They may be less comfortable determining the "right" thing to do, as opposed to analyzing the law and determining what is legal and what is not.

Compliance professionals who move into business roles bring with them the ethical chops and legal background to help the business thrive in a compliant way. There is a push to bring compliance professionals onto boards of directors in order to harness this experience. Moving from compliance into a legal or business-focused role can be a great career progression for those who like compliance, but think they might be better suited to legal or business work.

Compliance Consulting Work / Private Practice

Many compliance professionals enjoy "hanging out their own shingle" as solopreneur consultants or lawyers in private practice. Others join or create consulting companies or law firms that operate to serve clients.

Compliance professionals who move into law firm practice or consulting tend to love to work on multiple projects at once. They thrive on discreet work that can be delivered to the client, often with recommendations that will be implemented by the client – not the consultant or lawyer.

Those who successfully move into consulting or private practice must enjoy networking, marketing and sales. People in consulting or private practice must enjoy selling, because they must get the work, then retain the client by providing high-quality service, as well as selling new projects or being available to deal with new ligation or internal investigations.

Successful consultants and lawyers frequently bill by .10 of an hour, which can be a drag for many or feel deeply restrictive. The phrase, "the tyranny of the billable hour," comes into play here, as you will normally have a set number of minimum billable hours per year.

On the flip side, there is a higher income ceiling for consultants and lawyers in private practice than those working for a corporation. Hourly rates for highly specialized and respected consultants and lawyers can reach over $1,000 per hour, and firms that have been built into recognizable brands have sold for multi-million dollar sums.

In order to be a successful consultant or lawyer in the compliance field, it usually helps to have had at least one in-house role or experience from which to draw. If you start into consulting or law right out of school, you will want to do so with strong mentoring from people who have worked extensively in the profession.

One consultant's advice for getting into the field was to acquire, "A deep knowledge of behaviors and typologies identified by the regulator. Then network, network, network!"

Government

Another route many enjoy is working within a government function. Broadly speaking, there are two types of government roles: (1) working in an agency that performs a compliance-related function, or (2) working as a compliance officer for a government agency.

Government Agency Work

People working at compliance-related government agencies tend to work in prosecutorial or watchdog roles. Examples of such roles include people working for organizations that make or enforce anti-trust/competition laws (e.g., the European Commission), data protection regulators (e.g., the CNIL in France), and those that enforce trade sanctions (e.g., Office of Foreign Asset Control or OFAC in the U.S.).

Those who thrive in government agency work tend to enjoy rules and regulations. They also may enjoy having power and the ability to force companies to do the right thing or face the penalties their organization can impose. Government agency work can also come with great prestige, as people in business usually fear enforcement actors.

Working at a government agency can help you to move easily into a number of pathways afterward, including in-house corporate compliance work, consulting and private legal practice. Experience at a government agency is widely sought after. However, government agency work tends to pay poorly in comparison to both in-house and consulting/private practice work, which is a deterrent for some. Additionally, promotions may be difficult to come by, and the bureaucracy involved in many government agencies may put off the highly ambitious.

Compliance Officer for a Government Agency

Many government agencies have compliance officers working within them. For instance, the U.S. National Security Agency (NSA) has compliance officers who ensure agents adhere to the legislative mandate and court decisions governing NSA operations. All types of agencies, from the military to the local council, may have compliance officers.

Compliance officers working in government frequently have more job security than those working in the private sector. They also tend to receive better benefits and have access to secure pension plans that may not be available to workers outside of the public sector. The downside to these jobs is they aren't usually as well paid as those in the private sector or in consulting/private legal practice. Government agencies typically move more slowly than companies in implementing compliance programs. One government compliance officer's biggest complaint about her job was the "length of time it takes to fully implement process improvements."

Non-Governmental Organizations (NGOs) and Nonprofit Organizations

Another pathway for compliance professionals is work within NGOs or nonprofit organizations. NGOs and nonprofits tend to serve noble purposes. They tend to be dedicated to changing the world in some important way, whether for animals, people with diseases, or bringing about the resolution of conflict. Universities are also included in this category.

Working in compliance for an NGO or nonprofit can be deeply emotionally fulfilling, especially if you're lucky enough to work for an organization dedicated to a cause close to your heart. The downside of such work is that it tends to be lower paid than working in a for-profit corporation or in consulting/law practice. And because NGOs are largely unregulated (and infrequently prosecuted), the appetite to invest in compliance is sometimes quite limited.

Vendors

There are all kinds of vendors serving the compliance community. From online learning course developers to internal investigation firms, the number of vendors in the compliance community is growing every day.

Companies catering to the compliance community benefit greatly from the input of those who have already been in-house in a corporate or NGO/non-profit environment. Compliance professionals can be invaluable resources to vendors, as they know what compliance officers really want and can provide fantastic advice for product development and sales.

Working for a vendor can be extremely lucrative, especially if you join a technology-based company that offers stock or profit sharing. Not all vendors perform well, but those that do offer big opportunities.

On the flip side, many compliance professionals miss the day-to-day challenges of in-house practice when they work for a vendor. Developing products may not suit those who enjoy working on in-house problems; if you don't enjoy sales or product development, you're unlikely to thrive in a vendor environment.

In addition the broad categories above, there are other choices. Perhaps you want to work as an investigator, or as a health and safety inspector? Maybe you'll work in environmental compliance, workplace safety, products safety, privacy or become an import/export expert. The pathways are numerous, which makes the career choices broad and exciting.

So Which Path Should You Take?

As you can see, there are many pathways to get from where you are now to where you intend to go. Looking at the list above, is there one role that you think will fit you best? Maybe two appeal to you, and you can see how one might flow nicely into the other over a ten-year period. Choose one role to focus on so you can use the remainder of this book to position yourself as an expert in that field.

There is no one answer; each type of role has its plusses and minuses. Knowing what you value will make it easier to focus on the right role for you. For instance, if you love problem solving but hate sales, you may be cut out for NGO or nonprofit work. Perhaps you like sales and working on multiple projects – that may mean you want to focus on corporate compliance work for the next two years, then transition into consulting. By knowing where you want to go, you can maximize the opportunities created by where you are now.

Which of these career paths will make you happiest? According to my survey, all of them are likely to make you happy. Of all the people that responded to the survey, only 2% of people said they were unhappy they chose a career in compliance. 18% said they were sometimes happy they chose a career in compliance, which means fully 80% of survey responders said they were happy they chose a career in compliance. It doesn't matter what type of compliance you're in – you have an 80% chance of being happy in the career. Those odds are worth taking.

Which of these career paths will make you happiest? According to my survey, all of them are likely to make you happy.

Getting Into International Compliance

Every week or two someone emails me with the question: how do I get into international compliance? International compliance is sexy. You can travel to exotic places to do training, and you get to experience new cultures and food.

It is relatively easy to move into international compliance where I live in London, but in places where business is more likely to be regional, how can you prepare yourself for an international role, or position yourself to begin working on the international parts of your business? The key is preparation.

One of the major challenges in building a career is that employers always seem to want someone to already have the experience before hiring them into the role. The best way to create an opportunity for yourself before you've had the experience is to study up on the international laws affecting your industry before you interview for an international job.

Study the Laws that Affect International Compliance

Many practitioners become experts at the national laws affecting their business. Whether these are simple zoning regulations or complex healthcare laws like HIPAA, compliance professionals frequently become well versed at discussing national law. To work in international compliance, you must understand the laws of various countries and regions. Sound easy and obvious? It is, but it takes work and focus in order to learn something that you can't yet apply to your day job. Where should you start? I recommend:

UK Bribery Act: The UK Bribery Act is similar in some ways to the US Foreign Corrupt Practices Act, but there are dissimilarities that make the UK Bribery Act more stringent. For instance, facilitation payments are entirely banned under the UK Bribery Act. It may surprise you to learn that the UK Bribery Act sometimes applies in countries other than England, Wales, Scotland, and Northern Ireland. The broad reach of the UK Bribery Act means many companies can be caught if they operate in parts of the Commonwealth. Study up on the UK Bribery

Act so you can articulate the requirements, but more importantly, begin to think about how your business should respond to the complexities of the Act.

European Union Sanctions Laws: The European Union uses two different kinds of sanctioning instruments. One is called a directive, which "directs" each country in the EU to take the principles of the law and put them into their national legislation. The other is a regulation, which is immediately binding in its original form on all member states. EU sanctions are complex. Many include the names of individuals and entities with which companies in the EU are not allowed to do business. By studying the EU sanctions, you'll be able to flag issues that will come up in international business.

Data Privacy Laws: Perhaps the substantive area of law that most divides the US from the EU (and increasingly Asia and South America) is the area of data privacy law. Until US-based practitioners work in international business, many are unaware of the stringent data protection legislation in other parts of the world. Personal data protection is considered a human right in many places. One of the best ways to prepare yourself for an international role is to get an understanding of the European framework for the protection of personal data. Even better? Read up on the General Data Protection Regulation (GDPR). There is a shortage of data protection compliance specialists. By learning now, you'll prepare yourself for success later.

Anti-Money Laundering Obligations: The UK and EU have a wide range of laws and obligations relating to anti-money laundering. There is frequently personal liability for individuals who know or should have known about money laundering, and "know your customer" obligations are strict in many industries. By learning about international anti-money laundering frameworks (especially if your business has a financial services element), you can kick-start your career in international compliance.

The UK Modern Slavery Act: Like the UK Bribery Act, the Modern Slavery Act extends to businesses that operate outside the UK if they do business within the UK and certain thresholds are met. Prevention of human trafficking and modern slavery is critical for reputational protection. No company wants to be caught violating the rights of society's most vulnerable people. By reading up on your company's obligations under the Modern Slavery Act, you can increase your chances of becoming an international compliance professional.

Conflict Minerals and Import/Export: Depending on the remit of the compliance department, you may find yourself in charge of compliance with conflict mineral laws or import/export restrictions. If you work in the extractive industries, defense or technology, these are especially key areas of law to know.

Plan a Visit to Your Company's International Office(s)

If you want to get into international compliance at your current company, try to find a reason to have a business trip to an international office. Perhaps you can schedule your next meeting in South America or Europe? Maybe you can do your next internal investigation in person?

If there's no budget or reason to send you abroad, you can always plan your vacation to a place with a significant company office. Let's say you want your remit to expand to Europe or Africa. Can you plan a vacation to Spain and work one day in the Madrid office? Can you head to South Africa and meet the Cape Town-based legal and compliance team while you're there?

It may seem extreme to plan a visit abroad, but remember, people are always more comfortable with someone they know than someone they've never met. By making friends and alliances in the international offices, you are more likely to be invited to work in the international business section.

Write an Article on an International Issue for a Compliance-Related Magazine or Blog

I frequently help companies to hire the right compliance officer. Recently I was interviewing potential compliance officers to fill a role on one of my client's compliance teams. Several great candidates applied. One candidate had written an article in Compliance and Ethics Professional Magazine on a sanctions issue that was critically important to the hiring company. It probably won't surprise you that he got the job. The client was so impressed with the candidate's mastery of the subject (as proven by the article) that he immediately became the preferred candidate. If you want to move into international compliance, there's no better way to show thought leadership and understanding of the issues than to write about them in a public way.

It is advisable to ask experts to review your draft articles to make sure you have the law right. This can also build relationships and expand your network, while showing someone in the field that you're interested in getting into international work.

Get an International Certification

You may already be familiar with the Certified Compliance and Ethics Professional ("CCEP") qualification, but there is also an international version called the CCEP-I. You don't have to have worked internationally to sit the CCEP-International exam, but you do have to have experience in compliance. Gaining CCEP-I qualification shows that you have studied international compliance and understand the laws and requirements specific to working in multi-national organizations.

Another possibility is the International Association of Privacy Professionals' ("IAPP") CIPP certification. That certification proves you know about international privacy laws and best practices, which is critical for many international roles.

Network with People from the Countries in which You Want to Work

Want to work in Thailand? Great! Meet someone from Thailand at an international conference and stay in touch. Does this sound hard? Well, it isn't. The annual US National Compliance and Ethics Institute has an average of 1800-2000 attendees, with people from upwards of 30 countries. Seek out people from the countries and regions in which you'd like to work, so that you can more easily find out what's going on in their countries. Who knows – they might even tell you about a job and give you a good reference!

Apply for International Jobs

Does it seem far-fetched that a company might sponsor you to move to another country? It shouldn't – people move around the world for work every day. If you see a job at your company or on a website for a job in another country, why not apply? In many parts of the world, compliance officers are thin on the ground. Compliance is still nascent in much of Europe, Asia, South America, and Africa. Your skills and willingness to go to an unfamiliar country could take you on an incredible adventure. There's no harm in applying!

Study a Foreign Language

One of the biggest barriers to being hired to work internationally is a lack of language skills. You can overcome this barrier, and put yourself at the head of the applicant pool, by becoming proficient in another language. Choose a language based on either (1) the language in a country or region in which you'd like to work, or (2) the language that would most benefit your current business.

I took French in high school and studied Spanish in college. At the time I had no idea that I'd someday be living in Britain, and that one of my jobs would require monthly business trips to Paris. During college, I didn't know how much training I would be doing in Spanish-speaking countries, particularly in South America. My French is still quite rudimentary, and my Spanish is decent but not great. It doesn't matter – these language skills have allowed me to be comfortable when I'm traveling. More importantly, these skills have given managers faith in me and allowed me to be closer to the business because I quite literally "speak their language."

By investing in your further education, you'll be ready to jump in as soon as an international role is available. You'll also be able to convincingly discuss the international laws affecting your business and have an opinion about how to address them when you're being interviewed, and THAT can make all the difference.

Case Study: Tania Pavaskar on International Careers

Sometimes the best way to visualize a career path is to study someone who has already done what you want to do. Tania Pavaskar, Global Deputy Compliance Counsel in Singapore, has lived all over the world and successfully made a career in international compliance. She was kind enough to answer my questions for this book.

Kristy: You have an interesting background. Can you tell me about it?

Tania: I was born and raised in Mumbai in a suburb called Bandra, synonymous with Bollywood star sightings. I went to the University of Auckland, in New Zealand. My first job was at Proctor & Gamble in a purely commercial role with profit and loss responsibility for the largest region in New Zealand. After New Zealand, I went back to work in Mumbai and then Singapore.

Kristy: You've worked in a number of different industries. Did you find your skills to be transferable, or has each job required a new set of skills?

Tania: I have worked in fast-moving consumer goods, oil and gas, banking, mining, technology and publishing. My job at Proctor and Gamble was a terrific start to my career, as it prepared me to understand the commercial mindset and has been one of the most valuable roles in my journey so far.

The large mining company was looking for someone who understood the importance of health and safety. For my banking role, I had to learn a great deal about managing customer data and data privacy, and about compliance while dealing with higher regulatory requirements. My knowledge of health and safety, and later data privacy, are both transferrable skill sets.

In the banking role, I was responsible for understanding our licensing obligations. At the outset, that may seem miles away from FCPA compliance program design and implementation, but it has several similarities. With all types of roles, operationalizing compliance is a critical and often missed skill. More important than any skill is the requirement of a good attitude and desire to learn.

Kristy: How big a role does culture and diversity play in international compliance?

Tania: One would think that on a small island, the variety and diversity would be limited; however, Singapore is diverse because it is the APAC (Asia-Pacific) regional headquarters for most multi-national companies. One of my workplaces in Singapore had 27 nationalities working together, which is not uncommon in Singapore.

Kristy: What advice do you have for people looking to move into an international role?

Whether it's a change from a regional role to an international role, or a change of location, the key things are to:

1. Raise your hand: Often we underestimate the power of speaking up and showing interest. Let your interest be known.

2. Garner cultural awareness: An openness to learn a new culture without stereotyping anyone or anything will go a long way.

3. Find a role model: Figure out the type of career you'd like, and then seek out a person who is already living it. Ask them for their secret sauce, and for information on how they have walked in their professional journey.

4. Work effectively and earnestly: Your work ethic and enthusiasm will show when you bring rigor and momentum to every project you are involved in.

This and self-belief will help land that international role.

Raise your hand: Often we underestimate the power of speaking up and showing interest. Let your interest be known.

Chapter 4: Should I Take the Job?

Y ou've been pacing around the house for days. You've sent your resume, done your research, gone through an interview (or six), and now you're waiting for the call. Did you get it? Were you good enough? Then all of a sudden, the phone rings and... Congratulations! They're offering you the job!

After you've come off the initial high and had a glass of champagne to celebrate, it's time to make a decision. Should you take the job?

Considerations

Hopefully you've been asking questions along the way to help you to decide whether the job is right for you. You've probably considered whether or not the job is in an industry in which you'd like to work, and taken a peek at the regulatory and enforcement environment surrounding the industry. You've also probably gotten a sense of the salary, title and seniority level of the job. But these aren't the only considerations. Before deciding to take the job, think about the following.

Mandate

The Oxford English Dictionary defines mandate as, "An official order or commission to do something." Mandate comes from the Board and/or the C-suite. Having a proper mandate means you have been ordered to complete your duties, and more importantly, that the business has been instructed it must listen to you and do what you tell it to do.

Few things are more important than mandate. Noted compliance expert Donna Boehme says it is the most critical element of success in the job, and I agree with her. I have worked in companies in which Compliance has a strong mandate. Executing duties becomes relatively easy when this is the case.

If there is a strong mandate coming from the top, you'll be in good shape to succeed.

I've also worked with companies in a consulting capacity where mandate was lacking. Where mandate does not exist, Compliance is ultimately trying to ask nicely that requests be complied with. "Pretty, pretty please can you do the training?" is not anywhere near as compelling as, "Your team has 10 days to complete the training. The CEO has announced that failure to do so will be reflected in your bonus."

If there is a strong mandate coming from the top, you'll be in good shape to succeed.

Budget

Let's face it: you can't implement compliance without a budget. Technology solutions, online training, human resources and legal/consulting services make it possible to do the job well. One of my mentors described a company she was working at as "trying to make a compliance program using bubble gum and duct tape." That's not going to set you up for success.

If you don't have a budget that you control, you can't do the job properly. You must be able to do due diligence on third parties. If you have a lot of third parties, you'll need an online system to manage them, as opposed to an Excel spreadsheet. You need to travel to the territories in which your company operates, or at least be able to pay for webinar software or Skype for Business.

Budget is also important because it can limit or expand the compliance team. Try to ensure you have enough people on your team to get the job done. If you don't, you're setting yourself up to fail.

Other Resources

Think about the resources that you'll be given outside of budget. Has the company stopped supporting Microsoft Office in favor of the Google Suite because it is cheaper? Will you have access to administrative help? Does the company have a corporate travel agent, which will make your life easier when you travel? Think about the resources that you'll need to do the job effectively outside of budget.

Current Culture

Consider the feel of the office when you interviewed. Did it seem harried? Frantic? Calm? Were the people you met with in a terrible hurry, or checking their phones every two minutes? Did you like the person who will be your boss?

Corporate culture is within the remit of many compliance and ethics professionals. But before you decide to join a company, think about the culture as it is now. You'll be coming into the culture as it currently is, and it takes time to change that.

Bjarne Tellman, General Counsel at Pearson, talks about the challenges of what he calls a "legacy culture" in his book, *Building an Outstanding Legal Organization: Battle-Tested Strategies from a General Counsel*. I interviewed him on this topic for a blog I wrote, and he said:

"In legacy organizations, there is a culture already present, and replacing it wholesale is a fool's errand. However, it is possible to shift the existing culture, tilting it in a new direction, even if that can be a rather delicate maneuver.

If you push too far, too fast, however, you may damage the foundations of the existing culture, with potentially disastrous consequences. Instead of wholesale replacement, think of how you might prune a bonsai tree. You'd want to be very careful not to damage the trunk, which takes a long time to grow. Instead, you would prune the branches to gradually tilt the direction of growth, so that the shape of the entire tree changed over time, even though the trunk would remain firmly in place.

Applying that analogy to a legacy organization, you would want to consider identifying the core elements of the existing culture that need to remain and then identify which aspects of it you want to shape and influence. Focus on improving those parts of the legacy culture that are sub-optimal. The changes you are seeking are more iterative than revolutionary.

To do this requires that you first develop credibility and then seek to make changes when a suitable opening presents itself that enables you to leverage your credibility. Such openings often come at times of change, such as when the company enters markets or experiences financial crises or other setbacks. If you are new to the job, be careful about considering your arrival to be such an opening - you will have very little credibility in the first 100 days."

Culture change takes time – sometimes years. Do you want to work at the company in the meantime?

Who's the Boss?

There has been much debate within the compliance world about the proper place for Compliance to report. I agree with the stance of the SCCE and most experts that Compliance should report to the CEO and the Board of Directors. Compliance must be an independent function to be effective.

Many companies still have the Compliance Department reporting to the General Counsel or sitting within the Legal Department. The Legal Department has a different mandate than Compliance. Lawyers for the company must opine on whether actions are legal, not if they're right. Legal's job is to protect the company in a very different way than Compliance. Legal tends to favor settlement agreements, confidentiality, and quiet resolutions of potential issues. Compliance favors transparency, thorough investigations, and public resolutions that show the company is actively punishing wrongdoing.

Think about how you will be interacting with management. If the Board only hears about compliance issues via the General Counsel, it is not an ideal situation for you. There are outstanding General Counsels out there, and many are staunch advocates of the Compliance Department. However, if you can, join a company with a truly independent compliance and ethics function.

Will it Take You Where You Want to Go?

In the last chapter, we looked at a huge variety of roles and areas in which compliance professionals work. Hopefully you thought about where you'd like to go in the future – whether it's climbing the ranks in your current sector or moving to a new one.

I received an email from a young compliance professional who couldn't decide whether he should take a new job he had been offered. His email read as follows (some details have been changed to protect his privacy):

"I am currently a Compliance and Financial Crime manager at an insurance company in the UK. The company is a small, UK-only company; however, I have a fair amount of influence and am quite senior. I recently interviewed to be the Global Compliance Manager at a major cosmetics brand present in 63 countries. The role will be focused on anti-bribery and corruption, data protection, modern slavery etc. It is an exciting role, and I will be the only compliance professional within the company, so it is also very senior and influential. My concern is there is no financial services element, so it may pose challenges moving back into financial services at a later stage of my career. My current employer has countered with a fairly attractive offer; however, it still does not match up to the offer at the cosmetics brand.

I know you have a lot of cross-sector experience and have cited this as a good thing from a career progression perspective, so I would appreciate your thoughts on the above."

Like the Cat in Alice in Wonderland, it was clear to me that the correct answer to this gentleman's problem was entirely dependent on where he wanted to go. I responded to him:

"Thanks for your question, and congratulations! What an exciting time for you!

I think the move from a UK-only job into one that handles compliance in 63 countries is A HUGE step up. Also – if you'll be the only compliance professional in the company, that will give you a lot of experience in planning and executing the compliance program, which should set you up for having an even stronger resume in the future. Lastly, if the cosmetics brand is well known, people automatically give that brand awareness credence and find it impressive. It sounds to me like you should go for it.

But ... this depends on where you want your career to go. If your move after this one isn't back into the financial services sector, I think you'd find it hard to get back in. If your ultimate goal were to work in financial services compliance, then I'd recommend you stay where you are and start applying for more senior roles in banks or insurance. If you're married to financial services, I'd either (1) take this cosmetics job, while keeping your financial services network and expanding it, then take your next role back in finance, or (2) stay where you are, and start applying for jobs in the banking sector.

Here's the best news – either way, you're in a great position! GOOD LUCK! Let me know how it goes!"

He wrote me back a couple of weeks later telling me he'd decided to take the global role at the cosmetics brand.

There are no right or wrong answers for your career path. Consider the possibilities, and then build your contact base and experience to position yourself for your ideal role.

What's the Answer?

The truth is, until you join a company and spend time in the job, you'll never know what it's going to be like. You simply must weigh the considerations above, and then determine whether to leap into the unknown. Have courage, trust your gut, and remember – you can always get a new job if this one doesn't work out.

If you've decided to jump ship and take the new job – congratulations! It's time to negotiate your salary and benefits.

Chapter 5: Ask and it Is Given

Congratulations – you've accepted the job! While this is definitely a time to celebrate, you should also prepare yourself for the delicate art of negotiation.

Being offered a new job or promotion is exciting. There are new challenges ahead. You may be concerned you won't be able to get up to speed fast enough to be successful. Or perhaps you've been in an interim role for months and now you're being offered the opportunity to take the role on a permanent basis. Regardless of the circumstance, unless you don't want the role, you need to prepare yourself to negotiate.

Why You Must Negotiate

Many people make the mistake of taking the first offer they get. They get so excited, and so nervous that the employer won't negotiate, that they don't even try. They fear looking greedy or ungrateful, and are concerned that if they try to negotiate, the offer might be withdrawn entirely. I understand. I felt the same way when I first began negotiating my way into better roles.

In the past, when I was negotiating my job offers, I didn't realize how much the employer wanted me to say yes. They were frightened that I might decide I didn't want the role. They were concerned they'd need to start over again with the recruitment process, which costs huge amounts of time, money and lost productivity. The recruitment process is frequently long and tedious, full of interviews that don't work out and people who aren't what you thought they'd be. It's almost like dating. If you want to get married, you have to date, but kissing frogs is frustrating. You just want the process to be over.

However, when you're on the other side, trying to hire talent, you realize just how much power the applicant has once the role has been offered.

My first experience hiring people took place when I was in private practice at the law firm of Gibson, Dunn, and Crutcher. Every year Gibson Dunn had to compete against the other top firms for the best law students. I was asked to interview some of the law student applicants, and to take them to lunch or dinner to get to know them. If I thought the applicant would be a good fit for Gibson Dunn, the firm worked hard to convince the applicant that ours was the best place for them. It became highly competitive. We celebrated when a candidate chose our firm and felt terrible when they decided to go with one of the competing firms.

Later, when I was Chief Compliance Officer at United International Pictures, I was asked to interview the finalists and choose a junior attorney to come into the compliance department. I chose a fabulous candidate, who then negotiated her package.

The truth is, when the person I chose to be my junior attorney was negotiating her offer, I was terrified that we'd lose her. I'd spent two months interviewing OK but not great candidates. The junior attorney position was going to work closely with me, so I wanted someone not only with great experience, but also with a great attitude and a willingness to learn. I knew the person I'd chosen was the right person for the job, and I intervened on her behalf with HR to try to get her offer to a place where she'd be happy to accept.

This is all background to say, you have much more power than you think. Once the position has been offered, the employer really wants you to say yes. You're in the position to get what you want, or to come to an agreement with which you're both happy. How do you do that?

If You Don't Ask, You Don't Get

Here's the truth: if you don't ask, you don't get. In the fascinating book *Negotiating Your Salary: How to Make $1000 a Minute*, author Jack Chapman reminds readers that if you don't negotiate your offer, you won't get anything more than the original spec. However, if you negotiate, the worst-case scenario is that you end up with exactly the offer with which you began. So take heart – you can't be in a poorer position if you negotiate, so you might as well try to improve it.

Once you've resolved to negotiate your offer, it's time to consider what you want. People mostly desire more money, but don't forget that remuneration comes in many forms. Consider all of the different bargaining chips you have, which come both in monetary and non-monetary benefits.

Monetary Negotiating Items

Salary

The first thing you'll want to negotiate is your base salary. Try to get your salary as high as possible, as the number you come to will be the foundation on which all of your inflationary raises will be based.

Let's say you were offered $90,000 as your base salary, but you negotiated that up to $100,000. The following year, the company tells you that you're getting a 2% raise. If you hadn't negotiated, your salary would be raised by $1,800, whereas if you had negotiated, you'd have another $2,000 over the course of the year. If you extrapolate that out for ten years, your salary will be $121,899, instead of $109,709 – meaning you'll get over $1,000 more per month, simply because you negotiated in the beginning. Your base salary is the most important number you can negotiate.

Sign-On Bonus

When the market for compliance talent is tight, try to negotiate a sign-on bonus, especially if the company refuses to raise your base salary amount. Even if you're happy with the base remuneration, it never hurts to ask if you can have a sign-on bonus.

When I was considering moving from one of my jobs to another, I knew that if I accepted, I would be forfeiting my end-of-year bonus, which I had earned. I told the new company about the bonus that I would be forfeiting and asked them to "make me whole." They agreed to it, and I received the full amount that I would have received had I stayed in my old job.

Sign-on bonuses are more common when an area is in hot demand. If you know that talent in your area or with your specialties is scarce, try to get a bonus for leaving your current position and moving into the new company.

End-of-Period Increase

Another way to increase your salary is to pre-negotiate a time for it to increase if you achieve certain deliverables or goals. Let's say a company is concerned you might not perform up to expectations, or they've had a bad experience with the person previously in the role, and therefore they want you to prove your abilities before they give you everything they can. Negotiate the timeframe and parameters in which they require your performance. If you meet or exceed expectations, you will receive the raise. Try to position this as a win/win – you show your value to them and deliver what the company needs, and they give you a salary commensurate with the value you've already provided and will continue to provide.

Stock Options or Equity

One way to grow your wealth quickly is to become a partial owner of the company. The way you do this is through equity.

If you're at or going to a large publicly traded company, you may be able to negotiate stock options as part of your compensation. Stock options may be transferred to you immediately, given to you a little bit at a time, or conveyed to you all at once after you've been at the company for a designated period. This is called "vesting." Stocks can be traded or sold for cash, so these can be worthwhile.

Private companies may offer you ownership stakes as well. Partial ownership of an unproven or small company that pays a low salary in exchange for the opportunity to grow with it may be a useful strategy for you if you're able to take the gamble on a high return.

Retirement Contributions

Many companies are willing to give retirement contributions as part of their package. Companies like to do this instead of salary increases or other forms of remuneration, because they're often tax advantageous. Ask for a percentage of your salary to be automatically contributed by your company into your 401(k) account or pension scheme. This money won't be immediately available to you, but over time it can grow into the nest egg you'll need when you retire.

Non-Financial Negotiating Items

As you can see, there is more than one way to obtain monetary gain from your new position. But life isn't all about money and neither is negotiation. If a company has offered you the best financial package it can, you can also negotiate for other perks. These can include:

Title

Rightly or wrongly, people assume a certain level of seniority based on your title. If you're unhappy with the title offered, you can negotiate for a higher-level title. Corporations have different title structures. In some, "manager" or "director" is a higher-level title than "vice president." Try to understand the titles available and negotiate your way into the highest title you can.

Vacation Time

Time away from the office is critical for your sanity and enables you to do your very best work. My company requires employees to take their vacation time each year, because they inevitably come back refreshed and more creative. Vacation time is fantastic, because you're being paid not to be at work. Negotiating more time away can enable you to work on your passion projects, learn new skills, spend more time with those you love, or travel to new places.

Learning Budget

Many employers are happy to negotiate a budget to help you to learn new skills or to stay current on the trends and developments in the profession. You can negotiate this perk in different ways. Perhaps you can get the employer to commit to sending you to an annual conference, like the Compliance and Ethics Institute or an International Association of Privacy Professionals conference. Perhaps you can get an annual book or magazine budget, or a subscription to a newspaper. Maybe you can negotiate for access to online classes, or to have the annual fee paid for membership in an organization dedicated to compliance and ethics.

Negotiating for a learning-related budget has a dual benefit. Not only can you learn as you go in your current job, but you can use this new information to prepare you for a promotion or a higher-level job. Having a learning-related budget is a great perk, and one that should not be underestimated for its long-term value.

Flexible Working Conditions

Another perk you can negotiate for is flexible working conditions. Many people don't enjoy the traditional nine to five (or eight to six thirty!) that is expected of most full-time employees. Flexible working conditions can make a world of difference in handling the non-work-related parts of your life. Perhaps you can negotiate a certain number of days per week during which you can work from home. Maybe you can work ten hours, four days per week instead of eight hours, five days per week. Maybe you can start at 10:00 a.m. and finish at 6:00 or 7:00 p.m. instead of fighting the rush hour every day.

Some jobs may lend themselves to not working scheduled hours at all. If you're able to show your performance with deliverables, you may be able to negotiate a contract where you're not bound to certain hours, but are required to turn in materials by a certain date.

Flexible working hours can make a huge difference, especially if you have children or older parents who need your attention.

Location-Specific Perks

There are often location-specific perks for which you can negotiate. Does the building in which your office resides have a gym? Does it have a daycare or nursery? What about a canteen? Can you negotiate discounts or to have these perks included as part of your employment agreement? These types of perks can create a more convenient and comfortable working environment, and potentially save you money if you can cancel your gym membership or move your child's day care to one without fees!

Pre-Approved Writing and Speaking Opportunities

If you can, negotiate pre-approval for a certain number of writing or speaking opportunities. Many companies have strict policies limiting how many (if any) times per year an employee is allowed to attend a conference as a speaker or to write articles on topics related to work. By getting pre-approval to attend one or more conferences as a speaker each year, or getting permission to write one or more articles or blog posts each year, you'll guarantee yourself exposure within the profession without the challenges of negotiating each opportunity as it arises.

As you can see, there are many different chips you can use during your negotiation. Think of the different options as a recipe for success. You want to create a cake that tastes good to you. Perhaps you'd be happy with a carrot cake or a cheesecake, and both have many of the same ingredients. By picking and choosing which elements you need to be happy, you'll strike a great deal.

The next section is for the ladies, but gentlemen, feel free to read it as well. Women face special challenges when negotiating, so we'll address those issues next.

Chapter 6: Ask for It, Women's Edition

"Don't ever let someone tell you that you can't do something. Not even me. You got a dream, you gotta protect it. When people can't do something themselves, they're gonna tell you that you can't do it. You want something, go get it. Period."
-Will Smith (The Pursuit of Happiness, film)

The phrase, "Ask for it," when related to women, tends to stand for very bad things. Frankly, that is part of the problem. Women asking for what they want and deserve can be viewed extremely negatively in relation to work, promotions and opportunities.

In some ways, I'm discomforted including a section in this book specifically intended for women. At the same time, too much research has been done proving why women tend to make less money than men, and why we frequently progress less quickly in our careers than men, which makes this chapter necessary.

Why Do We have the Wage Gap?

In their seminal book, *Ask For It: How Women Can Use Negotiation to Get What They Really Want*, authors Linda Babcock and Sara Laschever explore the disparity between the genders in achieving earning parity. The research in the book boils down to this: most women fail to ask for promotions, higher salaries, better perks, and better mentoring, so they frequently fall behind their male equivalents.[1] Over decades, these 1% disparities can become 10% or 20% differentials, making the wage gap what it is.

Of course, failure to ask for what we're worth isn't the only factor creating the wage gap. For instance, women are significantly more likely to take career breaks than men to take care of small children, and women are more likely than men to be the primary caregivers to elderly parents. In Lean In, author Sheryl Sandburg notes:

"Although pundits and politicians, usually male, often claim that motherhood is the most important and difficult work of all, women who take time out of the workforce pay a big career penalty... Those who rejoin [after a career break] will often see their earnings decrease dramatically. Controlling for education and hours worked, women's average annual earnings decrease by 20% if they are out of the workforce for just one year. Average annual earnings decline by 30% after two to three years, which is the average amount of time that professional women off-ramp from the workforce."[2]

Regardless, there are some things that we can control more than others, and the first is that we ask for what we want. We need to ask for the promotions we deserve, for the salary we deserve, for the perks we deserve, and the opportunities we deserve.

We need to ask for the promotions we deserve, for the salary we deserve, for the perks we deserve, and the opportunities we deserve.

Applying for that Job or Promotion

A study referenced in Katty Kay and Claire Shipman's book, *The Confidence Code: The Science and Art of Self-Assurance— What Women Should Know*, showed that men will apply for a job or promotion if they meet 60% of the job qualifications, while women will apply for the job if they meet 100%.[3] Men tend to believe they'll grow into the new job, and women tend to wait until they have all of the relevant skills before applying.

The trouble with this thinking is that it holds women's careers back compared to men. If men are 40% more likely to go for a higher-level job than women, over a 30+ year career, men will move forward much more quickly than women, finishing their careers in higher positions.

What can we do about it? We can overcome our reticence by choosing to pursue promotions or jobs when we have 60% of the skills or experiences required for the job.

When I applied for the job of Director of Compliance at Carlson Wagontlit Travel, I had experience in anti-bribery work, anti-trust/competition work and data privacy. I had very limited experience in trade sanctions at the time, but I decided to apply for the job anyway. I had approximately 75% of the skills required, which made me nervous. I knew I didn't have 100% of the experience required. I'm so glad I went for it anyway.

I told the recruiter and hiring boss honestly that I didn't have sanctions experience, but I had all of the other required skills. I knew without a shadow of a doubt that I could learn whatever I didn't know at the time. They believed that I could learn trade sanctions because of my confidence. I didn't shy away from properly answering the question about my lack of background in sanctions work, but I didn't let that defeat me or make that a deal-breaker in the minds of the hiring bosses.

Resolve to go for it. If you have 60% or more of the skills required for a promotion that sounds interesting to you or a job you think you might enjoy, apply for it. Perhaps you won't get the job on the first try. That's OK. There are two benefits to going for a job you might not get. First, you'll meet new people and expand your network, even if it is only within your company. Second, you'll have more confidence because you'll realize that even if the answer is no, you've gained the experience that will help you to interview more effectively in the future.

When You Get an Offer, Negotiate

In the book *Ask for It*, author Linda Babcock tells the story of a plant biologist named Mary who was working at a large state university. She and six of her colleagues were asked to put together a grant proposal, which included salary requirements. She was outraged when she realized that all six male scientists were paid significantly more than her, including three junior scientists. While she was furiously writing her resignation letter, one of her male colleagues came in and talked to her. He was shocked to learn that she had never tried to negotiate her salary, but had simply taken the raises that were offered to her each year. Her male colleague said he always aimed to get at least 3% more than originally offered, which created a huge difference over time.

Mary went to the dean and demanded a $10,000 raise. The dean said he'd never thought Mary wanted more, as she seemed happy with the amounts she'd been offered, and then gave her the raise.

The moral of the story is that women tend to believe whatever offer comes to them is the best they can do. Instead of assuming that the offer is the starting point of negotiation, many women feel that it would be rude to ask for more, so they don't. Most companies expect candidates to negotiate, and therefore don't start with their best offer, lest they have no room to negotiate. Companies are, of course, obligated to maximize shareholder value and to try to gain the best deal that they can in negotiating with employees. If a woman takes the first offer, that's great for the company, but not great for the woman. Resolve that you will negotiate. Remember, even if you don't get more than the original offer, you won't be worse off; you'll just be in the place in which you started.

Explain Your Value

Many women have the philosophy that if they simply work hard enough, the boss or the company will see how much value they are adding, and they will be rewarded. Time after time, they toil and go the extra mile, only to be passed over in favor of the louder, brasher, ruder person who toots his or her own horn. The phrase, "the squeaky wheel gets the grease" is a cliché for a reason. The truth is, you must explain your value and talk about it in order for it to be appreciated, respected and rewarded.

Some of the best women I know believe everything should be fair. If they work harder or longer than their colleagues, that should be recognized and rewarded. In a perfect world, they are right. But we don't live in a perfect world, so they must learn to talk about their accomplishments and explain their value and contributions to their employers.

Adopt a strategy for sharing your accomplishments and contributions. Whether it's making goals, meeting those goals, and celebrating their achievement publicly, or simply noting in an email to your boss that you've accomplished an objective, be sure you have a consistent strategy for both sharing and celebrating your successes.

You need to be seen as a winner and as a person that can be counted on to deliver. Too many women consistently win and deliver on time or ahead of schedule, yet aren't given the kudos or promotions they deserve because no one is paying attention, or worse, managers simply come to expect the woman to perform without asking for more. Show your value AND be explicit in calling attention to it. By committing to this one action, you'll exponentially increase your ability to be successful.

Critical Times to Ignore Your Email

I'll never forget that Thursday night. I had been at board meetings for two days straight. I'd gone to the airport with the president of a crucial division of my company, and we were both in the lounge awaiting the flight. I had at least 100 emails to answer, but he was in a chatty mood. My brain told me to get out my computer and start responding to the emails, but instead, I listened to my heart, which told me that building the relationship with the leader was more critical than any email I might answer that night.

Later in the year, as things got tough within that division, the president was a crucial ally in getting the compliance agenda implemented. Had I simply gone to work answering email, I wouldn't have built the relationship that made it possible to fulfill my agenda and get the raise I deserved.

In her book, *Nice Girls Don't Get the Corner Office: Unconscious Mistakes Women Make That Sabotage Their Careers*, author Lois P. Frankel states that women are frequently so busy doing the day-to-day work that they don't do the relationship building that is critical to long-term success.[4] The cliché, "It's not what you know, but who you know," is very real. So many times we have the opportunity to get close to someone in power, but we're so busy doing our job that we forget that in the long term, relationships are much more critical than whatever email we put off until tomorrow.

Resolve to build relationships with people in power, even when you're busy. People in power are much more likely to go to bat for you, to mentor you, to champion you and to pro-actively help you manage your career if they know you personally.

Make your career development a priority. The commitment to doing so will produce real results.

Dealing with It's Not Fair

You may be saying, "But it's not fair! I shouldn't have to work harder or longer. I shouldn't have to kiss up to the boss or make strategic decisions to join networking groups or go to golf tournaments or happy hours. I should just be able to do my best work and be promoted based on merit." Yes, I agree. Now, back to reality.

It's not fair. And that's how it is (at least for now). By acknowledging this, and understanding that we can only change things if we are in positions of power, we give ourselves permission to do the hard work of self-promotion, asking for what we want, and playing the business game in a way that maintains our integrity but also puts our best foot forward.

It's maddening to know that your work is just as good as your co-worker's, and yet, that person gets promoted because he was willing to promote himself or talk about his contributions and value. Resolve once and for all that you're going to put your successes out there and publicly declare that you're important to the organization.

Always Raise Others Up as You Climb

One of my long-term goals is to mentor and fund up-and-coming female entrepreneurs. I recognize that I can only do that if my company is successful so that I have lessons to teach. Be the woman who rises so far up the corporate ladder that she has lessons to teach and stories to tell. You owe it to yourself, and also to the women who come after you.

Always raise others up as you climb.

Chapter 7: Moving Up the Ladder (or Jungle Gym)

"It doesn't matter where you are coming from. All that matters is where you are going."
- Brian Tracy

O nce you know where you want to go, it's easier to plan your career progression. One of the challenges of moving up is that the ladder is frequently undefined. In corporations, there is often only one person within the compliance department. If there are two or more, it's entirely possible your boss will work long beyond standard retirement age, making it effectively impossible for you to move up.

In law firms and consulting firms, partnership track gets ever longer, and many times older partners don't want to turn over their clients to the up-and-coming partners in preparation for retirement. Government jobs, with their rigid hierarchy and seniority-based promotions, don't give as much room for movement as corporate life.

But have hope – there are many ways to move up throughout your career, even if moving up means moving sideways before jumping to the next level. The question is this: is the best path for you the ladder or the jungle gym?

Moving Up Within a Defined Ladder

Despite the emergence of "flat" managerial structures in Silicon Valley, in many organizations there is still a strong hierarchical corporate ladder. Places with a defined corporate ladder tend to be more traditional and conservative, but that structure can also provide stability and a clearly defined role, which lets everyone know your position in the food chain.

How do you move up within the corporate ladder? The traditional way is to do your job well until your boss retires or moves to another company, but this can be boring and time consuming. Most of us want to move up fast. How can you improve your odds of promotion?

Actively Take More Responsibility

Find ways to take on more responsibility than you have right now. By the time a promotion rolls around, you will already have proven you have the skills and ability to handle it, because you've begun doing some of the tasks. Concerned you don't have the skills yet? Start slowly, taking on one new project or task at a time. In short, fake it 'til you make it. Act like you're confident in your abilities until you actually are confident in your abilities. Learning new skills can be difficult, but with some effort and courage, you'll become more and more effective at your job.

What happens if you've taken on a bunch of new responsibilities without a commensurate title or pay raise? First, talk to HR or your manager about all of the new responsibilities you've taken on in an effort to convince them to give you an expanded title and salary. If they still won't budge, you've still improved your position, because you'll be able to show new employers that you've already been performing at a higher level than you were previously.

Consider Certificates and Certifications

Another way to move up the corporate ladder is to obtain certificates or certifications. The most popular certifications in the compliance field are the Certified Compliance and Ethics Professional (CCEP) and Certified Compliance and Ethics Professional, International (CCEP-I) designations. These are offered by the Compliance Certification Board, which is run by the Society of Corporate Compliance and Ethics. Becoming certified not only shows your commitment to the profession, but also identifies you as a self-starter that is excited about advancement.

Another way to grow your skill set and the likelihood of promotion is to become certified in a compliance-related field. The International Association of Privacy Professionals (IAPP) offers certifications related to privacy. As European privacy law becomes more stringent and privacy regulations expand to have extraterritorial effect, more and more compliance professionals are required to take on privacy issues as well. Taking the initiative to obtain certifications and certificates (through classes) can prepare you to take on more responsibility, or to be prepared for another role.

Moving Up the Jungle Gym

In her book, *Lean In*, author Sheryl Sandberg states the latest way of moving up the corporate ladder may be by going sideways, swinging through different positions across, up and down, in order to ultimately climb upwards. Singular movement up the ladder is largely a thing of the past.

Climbing through the jungle gym to move your way upwards means moving to roles that may be at the same level but in a different area of the company. For instance, you may come in as a Compliance Manager, but then move to legal or import/export. The new knowledge you accumulate will make you a better candidate for the Compliance Director role, which has a broader base than your original Compliance Manager role. Even if the legal and import/export roles have the same seniority and pay grade, you will be in a better position to climb around the jungle gym.

What are some benefits of moving sideways before moving to the next level?

More Exposure to Leaders

Cultivating friendships with leaders can make you more likely to find a new position. The more people you know in the business, the more likely it is that when your name is brought into consideration for a plumb role or a promotion, you'll have backers and people who can vouch for your excellence.

You are also more likely to find a mentor or champion if you have a variety of experiences. Leaders talk to each other, and your good reputation will help you to curry favor in your new role.

More Exposure to the Business

The lynchpin of any successful compliance career is an intimate knowledge of the business, and the ability to determine how you can help your company get where it wants to go in a compliant and ethical way. The more you understand about the business, the more you can succeed in proactively offering the support it needs to grow.

Exposure to various parts of the business will help you to understand the organization in a more expansive way. When you go to your next role, you'll take with you the experiences you've had, which can inform your work in positive ways.

Greater Networking

Successful compliance officers build a network of supporters within the business who help them to get their work done. Meeting mid-level managers or rising-star employees in one area can be of huge benefit one or two years later when these employees move into more powerful positions. Likewise, when you build a network in one area of the business, you obtain the ability to introduce people in your new area to those in your last, exponentially improving the value of your relationships.

Greater Skill Set

The broader your experiences, the more likely you are to be hired into a more significant role than the one you currently have. When I decided to leave private practice to move into my first in-house compliance role, I had experience in anti-bribery work/corporate monitorships, anti-trust/competition, and data privacy. The role I applied for related to all these subjects, as well as extensive trade sanctions work. I was able to leverage my skills from private practice such that the company decided that I could learn how to manage trade sanctions.

When I applied for my next role, I was able to confidently describe not only my anti-bribery, competition/anti-trust and data privacy competencies, but also my knowledge of running a trade sanctions program. The skills expansion was key to me moving up.

Acquiring new skills and experiences can be the ticket to a whole new world of opportunity. Getting on the jungle gym and looking for new roles can be the route to all kinds of possibilities. Think broadly – you may want to jump out of compliance to expand your skills. Perhaps you can take a sabbatical from compliance working in sales. Legal, HR and audit are often great places to expand your skill set and your ability to collaborate effectively between functions. Look for opportunities to swing right or left on the jungle gym. Your next move may be straight up after that.

Going the Extra Mile Before You're Asked

"The habit of doing more than (one is) paid for is one which should have your serious and thoughtful attention ... The law upon which this lesson is based, would, of itself, practically ensure success to all who practice it in all they do."
- *Napoleon Hill*[5]

Are you in the habit of doing the bare minimum? Do you consistently wrap up at 5:00 p.m., even if important and time-sensitive projects are due? Do you find yourself saying, "That's not my job!" more than once every six months? If so, you're going to find it much harder to succeed.

Many people approach their jobs with the attitude that they'll give more when they get more. They'll network more when they are given a better title. They'll stay late and learn new skills after they receive a promotion. They'll earn the certification or take the course when their new role requires it. This is a recipe for slow career improvement, or worse.

Some people are so afraid of being taken advantage of that they refuse to work hard before they're sure that it will be appreciated. They approach each assignment as a battle and try to avoid doing anything that is not strictly in their contract. Unless they get overtime or other benefits, they avoid committing to expanded responsibilities. I have one friend who talked her way out of a big promotion by pushing too hard for unreasonable benefits and pay increases, because she was so afraid of being used. Instead of asking what she could do for the company for a fair return, she acted as if the company was "out to get her," and in the end, a consensus could not be reached.

Should you allow yourself to be taken advantage of? Absolutely not. If you've been working late every night for months with no end in sight, it is reasonable to ask for more help or more compensation. However, if you approach your job with the perspective of someone who wants to help and is a strong team player, you are much more likely to be promoted into a higher role.

I moved quickly from Director of Compliance into the Chief Compliance Officer role, and I'm certain much of that had to do with my commitment to being available, doing my best in every project, and being willing to learn and expand my skill set. Committing to growth and seeking out opportunity will move you up the career ladder or across the jungle gym faster than any other accelerant. The people at the top tend to get there because of hard work and commitment. When those people see themselves in you, they're more likely to mentor and champion you, and to pull you up with them as they rise up through the corporate hierarchy.

Knowing Your Numbers

One of the most frequent reasons for compliance officer failure is a lack of understanding of the numbers that reflect the trends of the organization.

It seems obvious that the compliance officer needs to be part of the business team, but without a basic knowledge of accounting and the most critical numbers, you're less likely to be considered a business asset.

Understanding the Business

You must understand the over-all sector in which your company operates. What are the trends affecting your sector? Is technology disrupting it? Is your sector stagnant? Is it growing quickly, or responding to pending legislation that may reduce business? Take time to answer these questions by reading a daily newspaper, following business blogs or signing up for email reports on the state of the sector and your business within it.

You must also understand where your country (or countries) are within the economic cycle. Markets and economies go up and down over the years, and knowing whether the economy is improving or contracting is critical for planning.

By having a solid grasp of the environment in which your business operates, you will become a much more valuable team player.

Knowing the Numbers

I've never thought of myself as particularly great at math. I, like many lawyers, joke that I went into law because I wasn't good with numbers. However, I've had to improve my skill set in that regard, as running a business requires the ability to understand balance sheets and profit and loss statements.

When I was a brand-new compliance officer, the first time I went to a big meeting of management, I felt like the finance guy was speaking a different language. "EBITDA was up 15% year-on-year," he said, and everyone nodded appreciatively. I sat there thinking, "E-bit -what??" Luckily, I was able to find a book in the library that explained the basic financial terms being used in the meetings. Over time I was delighted to begin to understand what was happening within the company. You owe it to yourself to understand the basics of business math so that you can credibly follow what's happening in the business.

If you work for a publicly traded company, you'll be able to access critical numbers in your company's 10Q and 10K reports. If you don't work for a publicly traded company, hopefully management shares their numbers and goals with you on a regular basis.

There are several "number" questions every compliance professional should ask, and find out the answers to, in order to be Wildly Successful. These are:

Where are We Now?

It's critical to know where the business is now. If you're publicly traded, it's easy to see the movement of the stock price. Just Google the company's name and "stock price," and you'll get a graph of the stock's movement over the past five years. If it's up, congratulations! Your management is probably happy. If it's trending downward, you may be in for a bumpy ride.

If your company is not publicly traded, try to find out how the company has been doing. Has it been paying bonuses? Has it been giving raises? Has it been laying people off or restructuring? Try to find out all you can about the current state of the business and where it hopes to go financially.

What is Our Revenue?

Revenue is defined by the Business Dictionary as "The income generated from sale of goods or services, or any other use of capital or assets, associated with the main operations of an organization before any costs or expenses are deducted." In other words, it's all the money the company brought in that year. Knowing the company's revenue is useful, because you can see how it improves or falters year-on-year. A company's revenue shows how much it sold.

Major investments, new product development, paying staff, and other costs will be deducted from the revenue to give you the next most important number: Profit.

What's Our Profit?

The Business Dictionary defines profit as, "The surplus remaining after total costs are deducted from total revenue, and the basis on which tax is computed and dividend is paid. It is the best-known measure of success in an enterprise." Profit is what's left over after salaries are paid, office rent is paid, and marketing costs are taken out (among other expenses). Profit is a critical number, because it tells you if the company made any money this year. Revenue only shows how much money came into the business. If costs exceed revenue, then the company won't have made any profit, which is a dangerous situation to be in.

Knowing the Plan

Once you've got a solid grasp of the numbers, your next task is to know where the business is going. What product lines are selling well? What new products are being developed? How is changing technology or other potential disruption affecting the sales and marketing plans for the company?

The more you know about where your company wants to go, the more you can be a strategic partner. If you know your company is expanding its online marketing efforts, you can choose to learn more about privacy law and global privacy compliance. If you know your company is expanding into politically difficult territories, you can take classes or attend webinars dealing with trade sanctions. The more forward-thinking you are about how you can contribute, the more successful you will be in adding value.

Winning Mentors and Champions

For years, you've probably been told that you need to find a mentor. Mentors are people you admire who can help you to navigate the challenges of your company or career because they've been there before. Mentors are important because they can see a bigger picture than you can. They've been there, done that, and they can help you to skip the mistakes they've either made or seen so that you can be more successful.

Mentors can come from within or outside your company. Usually they are in the same industry, but occasionally people are mentored by someone because they have something in common, such as living in the same geographical area, or being alumnus from the same school.

Perhaps more important than finding a mentor is finding a champion. Champions go beyond mentoring. Instead of simply giving advice to the mentee, they go into the business and promote their mentees to the leaders. Champions try to get you assigned to important projects where you'll have exposure to other leaders. They'll suggest you for promotions and provide references when requested so you have the best chance of advancing. Mentors can turn into champions, and are more likely to do so if you take their advice and implement it.

Four Rules for Winning a Great Mentor

Getting a mentor seems easy in theory, but can be difficult in practice. It takes vulnerability to ask for help and advice, and humility to be willing to listen. Potential mentors tend to be busy people. After all, you wouldn't be seeking mentoring and advice from someone who wasn't already highly successful. How can you stack the deck to win a great mentor?

Rule 1: Do your homework

Don't approach your potential mentor until you've done your homework on the person. The internet has made this infinitely easier than it used to be. Google and LinkedIn can be your best friends when you're seeking information on your potential mentor. First, track the person's career and look for anything they've written. If they've written a book, buy it and read it so you can talk about it with them. Have they blogged? Written for a magazine or been quoted in a newspaper? Find everything you can that they've created and be prepared to ask questions about it. They'll be flattered and impressed that you've taken the time to do this. Moreover, it will make it much easier for you to start a meaningful conversation that begins with depth, as opposed to saying, "Tell me about yourself," which will probably keep the conversation surface-level and may be met with annoyance.

Next – seek commonalities on LinkedIn. It's useful to find out whom you both know in common. But go beyond that. Look to see if you have similar volunteering interests. Did you grow up in the same part of the country? Try to find something to connect with right away. People like people who are like them and have something in common with them. Expressing a commonality immediately connects the mentor's past with yours, which will lead to a stronger relationship.

Rule 2: Have a Specific Request

There's a famous quote: "If you want something done fast, ask a busy person." Busy people tend to be quick-moving, motivated and action-oriented. They are usually happy to help, but can be irritated if you request "time for a coffee" or "to pick your brain." Several mentors I questioned said that nothing shuts them down faster than being asked "to pick their brain" when the potential mentee hadn't even done their homework first! Talking just to talk will not result in a satisfactory outcome.

Have a specific mission or request before you engage in conversation. For instance, would the mentor be willing to connect you to people in Wisconsin in the compliance industry? Would she review your resume and provide feedback? Would he give you tips on getting into the Executive Development program? When you have a specific, actionable request, mentors are much more willing to work with you, because they feel they can achieve something in helping you.

Rule 3: Plan Your Follow-Up Out Loud

When you've finished your conversation, tell the mentor how and when you'll be checking in or following up. This gives you two advantages: (1.) it tells the mentor that you'll continue to have a relationship with him or her and (2.) it gives you a powerful motivation to follow-up on the steps the mentor suggested. The more you take actions that follow the advice of the mentor, the more willing the mentor will be to invest further time in you. The more you continue to follow-up within the timeframes you set with your mentor, the more likely he or she will be to continue investing energy in your growth and career because you've proven you're worth it.

Ultimately, a mentor or champion wants to see that their investment in you helped you to succeed.

Rule 4: Say Thank You

Like everyone else, busy people want to feel appreciated. Be sure to say thank you for their time. Even better? When you say thank you, within the conversation mention something you learned or found fascinating to show you were engaged. It will make the mentor feel important and confirm that they made a difference in your life. Moreover, appreciation tends to be mutual. By thanking someone for their time and the way they made a difference, they will be more likely to want to see you again and to build the relationship.

Mentors and champions can make your career, but asking for someone's time and mishandling it will likely make the person avoid you in the future. Ultimately, a mentor or champion wants to see that their investment in you helped you to succeed.

Now that you've decided where you want to go and considered how you may get there, let's raise the roof on your profile so people know who you are.

Chapter 8: Raising Your Profile

Hiring and promoting people is an eye-opening experience. If you've never done it before, it's amazing to see how certain people stand out and others fade into the background. Sometimes it's not what you know, but whom you know. Other times, a candidate's innate passion for the profession is obvious because of his or her activities.

Whether or not you're currently looking for a job, it always behooves you to be seen as a leader in the field. How do you do that? There are several ways. Choose one or two and you'll find yourself better known and more likely to be thought of when a recruiter calls and says, "Do you know anyone who might be good for this role?"

Writing

When I'm asked what I recommend as the single best step a person can take to differentiate themselves in the field, I always have the same answer: write. Whether you choose to write a magazine article, blog piece, brochure or white paper, the act of writing does several things for you.

First, people assume that writers are experts. There's good reason for this assumption, as few people would write something related to their professional field unless it was thoroughly researched and based on facts or experience. People with highly sought-after expertise are frequently referred to as "having written the book on" the topic (even if that "book" is actually a blog post). If you want to showcase your expertise, there's nothing like putting it in writing to help people associate you with your area of specialization.

Second, publishing a blog post or article can help when you apply for a new job or promotion. When a recruiter, HR professional or hiring manager sees an article accompanying a job application that relates directly to the job's requirements, it shows mastery of the subject. I once had to sort through multiple resumes for a compliance officer job requiring extensive expertise in sanctions. One candidate included an article he'd written on changes to the Cuba sanctions program with his resume. That definitely caught my attention, and after interviewing, he got the job.

Not only can writing an article or blog show off your expertise, it can also show off your writing style. Few things distinguish a great compliance professional from a mediocre one more than the ability to write well. Compliance professionals must know how to write effectively. We're asked to draft policies and procedures, Codes of Conduct, training materials, and thousands of emails each year. Many of these emails are sent to senior managers, board members, or to all employees. Writing an article or blog post can show hiring managers that you're a competent and confident writer. In a world where writing expertise is in high demand, the ability to immediately establish credibility in this area is a major key to being hired.

What's Stopping You?

People often love the idea of writing but stop themselves before they even start. There are several reasons for this.

I Don't Know What to Write About

The first thing that stops people from writing is the idea that they don't know what they should write about. Some people can't think of any ideas that they like, and others think of one hundred ideas but can't choose one. Others pick an idea but can't get finished drafting an article because they second-guess themselves so much that they throw it away before it is finished.

You can write about a variety of topics, all of which will be valuable to the profession. These include, but aren't limited to:

- The latest enforcement action, and how it affects compliance programs
- New laws or proposed laws that may affect how programs will be run
- Trends that you see in the profession
- Best practices you've observed
- Benchmarking or responses to benchmarking surveys
- Case studies based on your own experience or the experience of others (with permission, of course)
- Information on topics related to professional development as applied to the compliance profession, such as:

  o Networking
  o Goal setting and planning
  o Persuasion and influence
  o Managing teams
  o Time management

    o   Career development

Once you begin writing, you're likely to see these types of topics all around you.

I Don't Know How to Write an Article

Once you've created a list of topics, choose one and commit to writing the article. I find it best to outline the article or blog post, then to write it out completely without any editing. Outlining helps me to know where I'm going, and it gives me a structure with which to work. Once I have my outline and structure in place, completing the first draft becomes a much easier task.

If you're having trouble with your topic, consider finding a co-author who can help you to fill in your knowledge gaps.

Most people find a sense of accomplishment in getting the first draft written. Editing is critical, but being critical of yourself and trying to edit as you write the first draft is a surefire way to ensure your article is never finished. Give yourself permission to "just" write, then go back and edit.

Logistics

Now for the logistics. The average article is between one thousand and three thousand words. Blog posts are even shorter, with an average of four hundred to eight hundred words. It's usually helpful to separate your thoughts into three to five major thoughts, which you can use as sub-headers.

You can write your article in a legalistic way, or you can go for a more conversational style.

What should the title be for your article or blog post? People love lists. By starting with a list of three to five points, you'll nearly always have a great article or blog post. Some great titles may be:

- The top five ways to [enter topic]
- Three great ways to [enter topic]
- [Number] of ways to avoid [enter topic]

Use this outline to help you get started:

[TITLE: ___ WAYS TO _____]

[Opening sentence(s) setting out the problem]

[Paragraph introducing why or how you've come up with a solution to the problem]

[Sub-title: Point 1]

[Paragraph about why point one helps fix the problem, followed by an example]

[Sub-title: Point 2]

[Paragraph about why point two helps fix the problem, followed by an example]

[Sub-title: Point 3]

[Paragraph about why point three helps fix the problem, followed by an example]

[Closing paragraph summarizing the three points and reiterating the ways in which the problem can be solved]

What if People Hate My Article or Disagree with Me?

There's no doubt about it. By sharing your knowledge or point of view with the world, you may receive negative responses. Sometimes people will disagree with your approach or conclusions, or sometimes they'll make comments that are intentionally hurtful or demeaning.

If someone disagrees with you, consider the source, and decide if the commentary is useful. Perhaps the person has a different point of view, or perhaps you've overlooked something that would have made your article better. Nothing is ever perfect, so try to learn from it and do a better job next time.

What if someone is very negative or insulting in response to your article? The first article I ever wrote for the FCPA Blog received quite a lot of attention, including a response from another so-called expert who emailed me to tell me why my point of view was wrong. As I continued to write, he'd take the opportunity to make negative comments about me everywhere from Twitter to LinkedIn. When other people would post my articles, he'd immediately chime in about how my writing was marketing disguised as thought leadership. His attacks felt personal. Ultimately, I blocked him from all of my social media sites so I couldn't see his comments.

Luckily, most people within the compliance community are collegial and genuinely interested in other people's experiences and ideas. Don't let fear of criticism stop you from writing. The profession needs to hear from you!

I Don't Know Where to Publish

There are many outlets in which to publish articles and blogs. Until people try, they usually think there's some kind of magic associated with being published. That may still be true for books, but for magazine articles and blogs, most editors are desperate for well-written content that they can publicize to draw traffic and enhance readership.

Try submitting to:

- Compliance and Ethics Professional Magazine

- The Compliance and Ethics Blog
- Compliance Next
- Compliance Week
- Ethikos
- FCPA Blog
- Compliance Kristy (my blog!)

You can also try submitting your work to specialist outlets like Entrepreneur, Inc., or other business-specific outlets.

Another great way to get published is to focus on vendors that produce magazines, blogs, white papers and other publications. Many technology-oriented vendors attend conferences like the annual Compliance and Ethics Institute. If you go to the exhibit hall to meet the exhibitors, you can ask them about submitting for their blogs. This approach has enabled me to publish pieces for and with Steele CIS, Trace International, NAVEX Global and many others.

I've also met editors of compliance-related magazines and newspapers at conferences. They've been a huge help to me. For instance, I met Ben DiPietro from the Wall Street Journal, at the Compliance and Ethics Institute. He and I stayed in touch, and when my first book came out, I sent him a copy. He did a Q&A with me in an article on the book that ran in the Wall Street Journal, Risk and Compliance section.

It's easier than you might think to meet editors, social media managers and publishers within the compliance field. Write a great piece, find an outlet, and you too can go by the title "published expert" in the field.

Speaking at Conferences and Events

Besides writing, there is nothing like public speaking at conferences and compliance-related events to raise your profile dramatically. Some people fear public speaking more than they fear death (leading to the phrase, "I'd rather die than..."). While the fear is real, preparation can make a tremendous difference in enabling you to have a great presentation. If you're afraid, practice. Practice can make you better, as can studying those who speak well.

Speaking in public can boost your career in myriad ways. First, simply being in front of people shows you are a leader and expert in your topic. When you get up in front of others, you assume the role of teacher or professor, and the notoriety can make you a mini-celebrity at the conferences you attend.

Next, speaking can make you more knowledgeable about your topic. Preparing for a speech requires thinking through your topic, creating an outline, researching your points, drafting your slides and practicing. By the time you give your presentation, you will have learned much more about your topic than you knew before, which can lead to even more opportunities.

You never know where a speaking presentation might lead. I was talking to Joe Murphy at a conference one time, and he off-handedly said that he'd love to see a presentation on selling compliance to the business. I thought his idea was fascinating, so I submitted the idea for a session at the European Compliance and Ethics Institute. When my proposal was chosen I thought, "Oh shoot! Now I have to learn and present on this!" I spent the next three months reading about sales techniques and influence, then wrote and performed the presentation. The response was great, and I was asked to perform the speech at the International Compliance and Ethics Institute. The speech became the basis for my first book, *How to Be a Wildly Effective Compliance Officer*. You never know where a speech may take you!

So What's Stopping You?

I Don't Know What to Speak About

When trying to come up with a topic for a conference or event presentation, you can follow the same pathways as when writing an article. These include:

- The latest enforcement action, and how it affects compliance programs
- New laws or proposed laws that may affect how programs will be run
- Trends that you see in the profession
- Best practices you've observed
- Benchmarking or responses to benchmarking surveys
- Case studies based on your own experience or the experience of others (with permission, of course)
- Information on topics related to professional development as applied to the compliance profession, such as:

  - Networking
  - Goal setting and planning
  - Persuasion and influence
  - Managing teams
  - Time management
  - Career development

I'm Not Sure in What Way I Should Present

If you want to, you can perform your session by yourself. You can also perform with a partner or two, or do a presentation as part of a panel or as the leader of a panel.

There are pluses and minuses to each type of presentation.

Solo Performance

Plus: If you perform alone, you are the only person in the spotlight. You can control the pace and content of your presentation, and can include all of the material you think will be useful. You don't have to worry about other people's presentation style. More importantly, you don't have to worry about anyone else eating up your time, going over, or not preparing properly for the presentation.

Minus: If you make a mistake or don't perform well, an hour can seem like a really long time to keep going. There's nobody else to lean on if the session isn't going well. You also have to have your timing down so that you don't finish too early or have material left over at the end.

Two or Three Presenters

Plus: Multiple presenters are usually more interesting than a solo presenter because the audience is able to hear more than one point of view. As everyone has different career experiences, invariably the presenters will show diversity in their approaches to challenges. More than one person usually makes lighter work of preparation, as more than one person is involved in making the slides or deciding the content. Additionally, if the session isn't interesting, you can always start a discussion to make it livelier.

Minus: Many sessions with more than one presenter have timing issues. Someone will speak too long, which can throw off everyone else. You may also disagree on how to approach a topic. Sometimes people agree to do a session, then find themselves too busy to properly prepare, leaving a co-presenter to do the work.

Panel Sessions

Plus: Panel sessions allow multiple people to give their thoughts conversationally, instead of in a lecture format. Panels usually consist of one moderator and two to four participants. Ideally a panel will provide multiple points of view on a subject, utilizing each person's unique experience. Panel sessions can be less stressful than lecture-style performances, as they don't require the same level of preparation or practice. They can also be easier because there are so many people available to carry the burden of performance.

Minus: Panel sessions may fail to showcase your true expertise or experience, because there are so many people clamoring to get a word in edgewise. Someone else may make the point you were hoping to make. Oftentimes one person will dominate the conversation, leaving others unable to contribute as much as they would like. Panel sessions can also be dreadfully boring if the participants don't come prepared to tell stories.

I'm Afraid I Will Be Boring, or I Won't Do a Good Job

Pubic speaking can feel like standing in front of an audience naked. It's easy to be intimidated and to have nightmares about it all going wrong. However, there are some tried and true ways to ensure your presentation is as good as it can be. The number one way to ensure your presentation is good is to practice it. Experts believe running your speech three times out loud is the best way to ensure its success. Besides being prepared, there are many other ways to ensure your presentation is memorable and useful to the audience.

How to Make a Great First Impression

Most compliance presentations I've been to have dreadful openings. Whether it is a board meeting, training session or a conference presentation, nearly all of them start out with something along the lines of, "Thank you for being here," or "My name is Kesha Smith and I'm here to tell you about the FCPA..." I have some bad news. It's already too late. You've lost the audience.

Some social scientists believe that humans have devolved to have attention spans shorter than that of a goldfish. Most estimate that presenters have between 30 and 60 seconds to engage an audience. Within that opening time, members of the audience will decide if they are interested in listening to you. To grab the audience's attention, you can:

Start with a Question

By beginning with a question, you immediately bring the audience into the presentation. You're asking them to become involved, and to give their opinion or bring their thought to the topic. Even if you ask a rhetorical question that you don't expect them to answer out loud, by asking a question you immediately invite participation, which will make them more likely to listen.

Put Up an Illustration or Picture Without Text

People love puzzles. By starting with an unexplained picture, people will try to figure out why you put up the picture. Illustrations or funny quotes can bring people into the presentation quickly. If a picture is worth a thousand words, start with one so your presentation can be shorter.

Begin with a Story

People love stories. To make this tactic especially effective – tell the story in the first person or begin in the middle of the story. Have you ever noticed how many novels begin with something like, "It wasn't supposed to come to this. Jan was in jail, and he knew why..." Tell a story and begin in the heat of the action. People will want to know how the story begins and ends.

Do Something Unexpected

Carmine Gallo, the author of the book "*Talk like TED*," tells a story about how Bill Gates engaged his audience during his TED talk. Mr. Gates was talking about how malaria vaccines and medications were needed, and how vulnerable a population is without them. Gates opened a bell jar saying that there were mosquitoes in it, and then explained to the room that they shouldn't worry, only some of the mosquitoes carried malaria.[6] You can imagine how visceral the response was from the audience. Your action doesn't have to be that dramatic, but by creating an unexpected moment for dramatic effect, you can truly engage your audience in your story.

Why is it critical to have a great opening? Because you're much more likely to have a great close when you grab the audience's attention from the beginning.

Congratulations! You've started well. Now what? Well, that depends on whether you're performing in a lecture-style session or on a panel.

I'm not Sure How to Do a Good Lecture-Style Session

There are many great ways to perform a lecture-style session. As noted above, you can involve the audience, tell great stories, pace your session well and ensure the content is appropriate for the audience. There are also ways to ruin a presentation. To be Wildly Successful...

Don't Put Everything You Know on the Slides

I understand – you're a subject matter expert. You really, really, really know your stuff. It feels impossible to cull it down into just the essentials. Plus, slide 16 doesn't give all of the exceptions to that law. Maybe it should be two slides ... STOP. STOP RIGHT NOW.

Lawyers, perfectionists, and compliance professionals frequently struggle with the curse of needing everything to be entirely complete. Instead of focusing on what the audience needs to know, we focus on giving them everything we know. This creates audience fatigue. The audience only wants to hear what they can use, so putting everything you know on the slides can turn off an audience immediately. Instead, only put a few words on each slide to remind yourself of what you need to tell them verbally.

Don't Skip Slides Mid-Presentation

This is my number one pet peeve. I'll be watching a really good presentation where the speaker is clearly knowledgeable, then all of a sudden she'll say something like, "Wait, I'm running out of time. I put these slides in so you can have all of the information and you can read them later (skipping past five slides)..." If the information is important enough to the presentation to be included in the slides, then why is the speaker skipping over them?

Maybe you have a better attention span than I do, but I tend to spend the next five minutes after the slides were skipped trying to figure out what was in them and why they were skipped.

If you need to put information into your presentation that you don't plan to discuss live, put the information either into the notes for your slides or into an appendix. Putting together an appendix of useful information makes everyone happy. Also, this approach ensures your audience doesn't go away feeling angry that you didn't impart the information they came to hear.

Don't Forget to Calculate the Time Your Slides Will Take

There are very few things more annoying than a presenter spending 25 minutes going through the first six slides, and then rushing through the next 15 to try to finish on time. If you have an hour and you've created 30 slides, then you have an average of two minutes per slide. If you have 30 minutes to present and you've created 52 slides, you've created a giant problem for yourself! Edit down the slides and present the critical information in a timely fashion.

If you have 30 minutes to present, and you've created 52 slides, you've created a giant problem for yourself!

Pro tip: calculate exactly how many minutes you should average per slide, and then practice with a timer so that you know what one minute and five minutes feel like.

Don't Use Small Font

So, the latest court case's opinion used 250 words to expertly describe the newest FCPA-related nuance... this does not mean that you should write out all 250 words in tiny font so it fits on one slide. Please – do NOT use 20 words where three would remind you what you wanted to say.

There are at least two problems with small print. Number one – people get extremely frustrated when they see the screen but can't read the words. Number two – people ignore what you're saying while they try in vain to read the words.

Well-meaning practitioners think they're doing their audience a favor by adding the entire text of a quote or a decision on the screen when everyone can't read it. They are not. Small print frustrates the audience and takes away from the message.

Don't Read the Text Off the Slides

I'm loath to even include this point. But no matter how many times I see this advice, there are at least twice as many presentations where I see someone reading off their slides. There is no reason to read off your slides. If you want to use a quote, show the picture of the author and read it off your notes. Use bullet points to trigger your memory. But please, please don't read your slides to the audience. Chances are good that your audience is very bright and educated. They can invariably read faster than you can speak, so use this to your advantage and make your presentation more interesting by using animations to slowly reveal your main points or to bullet your key takeaways.

I'm not Sure How to Rock a Panel Session

Panel sessions require different planning and preparation than a lecture-style session. In order to rock your panel session:

Ensure Proper Introductions

A good panel moderator will prepare a short introduction for each panel member. If you are the moderator, email one-minute of introductory text to each participant to ensure you're focusing on the most relevant parts of his or her career, and invite participants to edit it.

If you're on a panel and the moderator is winging it, be sure to send a three-to-four sentence paragraph to the moderator laying out your introduction. You don't want to be surprised, and more importantly, you want to ensure your most critical biographical information is presented. If the audience doesn't already know your relevant experience, they will be less inclined to listen than if they are primed to be impressed.

You Never Get a Second Chance to Make a First Impression

If you are the moderator, be sure to prepare a first question for each participant that will showcase one of his or her areas of expertise. Too many moderators ask open-ended questions like, "So Joe, tell me about your experience..." or "Sheila, I understand you run a compliance program. Tell me about that..." These questions do not set panelists up for success. Create an experience-specific question for panelists, and send it to them beforehand, so they can start successfully.

If you're on a panel and the moderator hasn't sent you an opening question, don't be shy about sending a couple of choices to the moderator with a note saying, "I love the topic about which we're speaking. I was thinking it might be good if you ask me one of the following questions so we can spark a discussion right away..." You'll be doing yourself a favor, as well as the moderator.

Ask and Answer the Questions the Audience Wants to Ask

I once had the privilege of seeing Oprah Winfrey speak on stage at-length about her career. When talking about the success of her show, she said she wasn't just a naturally gifted interviewer – she always put herself in the shoes of her audience and asked the questions they wanted to ask. She was always polite, but she didn't shy away from asking the tough questions the audience would ask if they had the microphone.

Too many compliance-oriented presentations are banal discussions of comfortable talking points. If you're the moderator, ask the questions the people in the audience are asking in their heads. If you're on the panel, think about what the people in the audience want to know and then preface the discussion with statements like, "I know you may all be wondering..." or "If I were in the audience, I'd want to know..." By acknowledging what the audience wants to know (even if it is difficult to discuss or is controversial), you'll engage with them on a deeper level.

Ask the Audience

While it is important for moderators and panelists to anticipate what the audience wants to know, there's nothing like asking the audience for their questions and answering them directly. If a panelist makes an interesting statement, audience members may want to follow-up with a question. Skipping the Q&A can frustrate the audience. If you're a moderator, ensure that at least 10 minutes is dedicated to this task. If you're a panelist, look at the audience and offer to answer questions toward the end of the presentation.

Prepare for Silence

As important as it is to allow the audience to ask questions, sometimes the panel will be met with silence. Perhaps the audience is shy and doesn't want to appear unknowledgeable around their peers. Perhaps the audience is bored and already knows the information you've been discussing. No matter the reason, there may be times when the audience doesn't want to ask questions. In this case, it is critical that the moderator have a list of pre-determined topics to bring about discussion between the panelists.

If you're a panelist, prepare two or three questions for your co-panelists so that you can facilitate discussion if a dreaded lull occurs within the presentation. The audience may not realize you're saving the day, but the presentation will keep moving and remain relevant because of your preparation.

Panel discussions can be riveting and fascinating, but they require correct preparation and proper flow to be engaging.

Dealing with Negative Reviews and Comments

Every time I speak at a conference, I know the day will soon come when I receive the dreaded email detailing feedback from the audience. The first time you perform in public, you may be excited to get your comments and reviews. If you're lucky, they'll mostly be positive or constructive. However, along with positive and constructive responses, you're likely to have one or more negative or destructive responses. Let's put reviews and comments into perspective.

Try not to Focus Entirely on the Negative

What is it about human nature that loves to focus on the negative? In response to my first big keynote address, I had 110 positive comments (my husband counted) and 22 negative ones. I quickly read through the positive comments, not stopping to internalize or appreciate them. I found the negatives, many of which stung. One of the themes of my keynote was the message that compliance and ethics officers are part of a movement changing the world. One person wrote, "For me it was contrived and felt fake. I'm a realist and know in my 16 years in ethics and compliance that we can make a difference, but we are not changing the world." A couple of others accused me of being egotistical, shouting, and being self-promotional. Ouch.

A speaker will never be able to please everyone. If you're energetic and interesting, you will invariably annoy someone who likes traditional presentations. If you're stoic and facts-focused, you'll lose the millennials and those who want to be entertained. Understand that not everyone will like you, and that's OK. Take time to internalize the positive comments, and try to give them at least as much weight as the negative ones.

There are two questions you should ask of yourself when reading negative comments.

Can You Ignore It?

Newscaster Megyn Kelly said, "Reading negative remarks about yourself online is like breathing bus exhaust. With each one you read, you let your detractors steal your mojo. Life's too short for that."[7]

Whether in anonymous internet forums or on evaluation forms, people feel great freedom to criticize when they don't have to look the person in the face to deliver their appraisal. Some people get a sense of power from tearing others down when they can hide anonymously behind their computer screen. Try to ignore purposefully hurtful commentary. If the review isn't meant to be helpful or constructive, ignore it.

Can It Be Useful?

It's also useful to remember that criticism can be constructive and make you better. Jack Canfield, the author of The Success Principles, encourages readers actively to solicit feedback. When I read that I recoiled – why would I ever want to actively seek out criticism?

Canfield compellingly makes the case that we can never grow as people or in our profession unless we are alerted to the areas in which we can improve. He states that most people will be tentative in giving real feedback at first, expecting a defensive response to their honesty.[8]

However, if you can overcome the natural instinct to defend yourself, and instead internalize the pieces of constructive criticism that are useful, people will begin to be confident in giving you feedback, which will help you to improve. When I decided to actively seek out feedback and stop taking it personally, I allowed the responses to be a pathway to improvement, and I grew in my abilities.

When I decided to actively seek out feedback and stop taking it personally, I allowed the responses to be a pathway to improvement, and I grew in my abilities.

Try to Internalize the Positive

While evaluating negative criticism can be useful, never forget to spend time enjoying the positive feedback you receive. No one is universally liked, and no one approach will work for all people, so it's only natural that some people will like the way you communicate or the training that you give, and other people will not. By internalizing the positive statements people make, you can continue to do the things that are working. This will make you more effective.

Criticism can help you to build up your skills or tear down your self-esteem – the choice of what to internalize and how to use it is up to you.

Building a Wildly Successful career isn't just about raising your profile. It's also about joining in with other professionals to build your skill set, knowledge and network. How do you do that effectively? Let's find out.

Chapter 9: Join in, Everybody's Doing It

After speaking and writing, another great way to raise your profile is to join one of the myriad organizations that exist to support the compliance and ethics community. Organizations range from international non-profits to volunteer-based groups. Some groups are simply friends gathering together every other month to get lunch and talk about how to resolve their compliance-related problems.

The Benefits of Joining In

Compliance officers are perpetually busy people, but in my opinion, you don't have time not to be involved with at least one organization. When you join in, you'll:

- Have a group of people with whom to benchmark your program
- Have a group of people who can give you feedback on your initiatives and ideas
- Have a place to vent your frustrations
- Have a place to learn about new laws

- Have a place to learn about new legal cases and regulator expectations
- Have a place to discuss best practices
- Have people with whom to co-write an article
- Have people with whom to co-present a presentation or to invite onto your panel
- Know people to recommend for new jobs
- Know people to bring into your company when a new job is open
- Know people to help you get your next job

Joining in can be tricky, especially at first. So what kind of organization should you join?

Large International Nonprofit Groups

Groups like the Society of Corporate Compliance and Ethics (SCCE) and the Ethics and Compliance Initiative are large international organizations created entirely to promote the compliance and ethics profession. I am on the Board of Directors of the SCCE, and I'd highly recommend the organization to anyone interested in compliance and ethics as a career.

Large international groups have the benefit of scale. Everything they do can be done on a large level. For instance, the annual SCCE conference in the fall typically has around two thousand attendees. There are ten different session tracks for different professional needs.

The downside to the large size of the SCCE, Ethics and Compliance Initiative, and others is that it is easy to feel lost in the group. Unless you proactively work to make friends or to be involved, it's common to not feel a part of the organization, and to lose interest in it.

Smaller or Local Nonprofit Groups

Smaller nonprofit groups can be a great way to meet other compliance people in your area. Some, like the Bay Area Ethics and Compliance Association, are local groups, while others, like the Women in Compliance, focus on a specific niche in the compliance realm. In London, where I live, there is a group dedicated to Women in Regulatory Law that includes lawyers in private practice as well as those working in-house in regulatory compliance roles.

These groups can be fantastic places to network and to meet people who may become both colleagues and friends. The downside to these groups is that they sometimes become exclusive or clique-y, which may dissuade others from fully participating if they don't feel welcome.

For-Profit Industry Groups

Many companies within the compliance community host events and get-togethers for members of the compliance profession. Technology companies like Steele and NAVEX host in-person events in major cities, as well as the online Compliance Next community. Compliance Week hosts conferences and events in the United States and Europe, and technology and training companies from Convercent to SAI Global host roundtables and sharing sessions.

When I was a Chief Compliance Officer, I attended a quarterly get together of other CCOs that was hosted by PriceWaterhouseCoopers (PWC) in London. These get-togethers proved invaluable for me, as I was able to learn from CCOs with more experience and share what I was learning in my company.

The benefit of for-profit industry groups and events is that they tend to be hosted in nice places with high-level colleagues. They are usually free, which can be great for compliance officers without a learning budget.

The downside to these groups is that the events tend to come with a big dose of sales pitch, and you may feel implicit pressure to use the product. Worse, you may only be invited if you use the product, and may be chucked off the invite list if you stop using the service.

OK, I've Joined. Now what?

No matter what type(s) of groups you get involved with, there are many ways in which you can participate. Joining is only half the battle. By participating you can raise your profile, increase your network, and get more out of the organization than if you're a casual observer.

Here are ten ways you can get involved in your favorite organization. Not every way will apply to every group, but if you try, you can definitely find a way to meaningfully participate.

Writing

As we discussed previously, writing is a great way to share your knowledge and expertise. Draft an article or blog post on any compliance-related topic for publications sponsored by your group. It will be seen by members of the organization and can be used to boost your career by showing your knowledge to the outside world.

Speaking

Speaking is a great way to share your knowledge and to participate in the discussion about regulatory expectations and best practices. There are many outlets that you can use for speaking. For instance, at the SCCE, you can submit a topic for:

- The National Conference
- Regional Conferences
- Specialist Conferences
- Webinars

You can also volunteer to introduce a speaker at a conference, which can help you ease your way into giving a full session.

Referring

For most organizations, the best endorsement is a referral from its members to others in the compliance community. You can refer by:

- Forwarding emails regarding academies, conferences, and other events
- Telling your friends about the events you've attended and suggesting they come along next time
- Bringing your teammates and colleagues to the next event with you or sharing what you've learned with them

Sharing Content

An easy way to get the word out about your organization is by sharing the content that it or its members produce. You do this by sharing links to a blog or website via social media channels. This includes:

- Sharing on LinkedIn in your personal news feed
- Sharing on LinkedIn in groups dedicated to compliance
- Sharing on Facebook in your personal news feed
- Sharing on Facebook in pages dedicated to compliance

- Tweeting links to content via Twitter
- Sharing on other social media sites, such as Google+, Instagram, and Pinterest

Certification

A major purpose of the SCCE is to allow compliance professionals to become certified to confirm their knowledge and experience. Other organizations offer certification as well. You can promote your organization's certifications by:

- Linking your certified status within your LinkedIn profile
- Linking your certified status within your email signature
- Proudly displaying your certificate on the wall of your office or home

Conference Activities

Many organizations hold conferences which include opportunities to connect outside of the sessions. Where available, you can:

- Join in the networking events or coffee breaks to meet others in the field
- Join in mentoring events to either mentor people within the compliance community or become a mentee
- Go to the yoga class or participate in the fitness challenge
- Join in related volunteer activities
- Provide items for or bid on items in the silent auctions

Socializing and Support

Compliance work can often be lonely, so one of the best ways to stay involved is to:

- Offer support for the people who work within the field

- Connect with new members online via sites like LinkedIn to welcome them to the profession and the organization
- Stay in touch with people you meet at conferences and academies

Providing Feedback and Reviews

Organizations creating conferences and publications want to know what works and what doesn't. One way you can help is to provide reviews and feedback. You can do this by:

- Reviewing books and materials about compliance on Amazon.com, Goodreads.com and other review-based websites
- Providing feedback on the sessions you attend at conferences on feedback forms, both to evaluate the speakers and the content/topic of the session
- Answering the surveys put out by the organization

Supporting Vendor Relationships

There are terrific vendors supporting the compliance community. Consultants, lawyers, online learning platforms, internal investigation trackers, due diligence providers and others make the lives of compliance professionals easier and allow programs to run more efficiently. If you have a vendor that you love that would be beneficial to the community, encourage them to:

- Exhibit at your organization's compliance-related conferences
- Advertise in your organization's compliance-related publications
- Perform in a webinar where they share their expertise and best practices

Running for the Board and Other Offices

Most volunteer organizations require strong leadership and people with vision to grow the group. Once you've been involved with an organization long enough to know the leaders, consider running for an office or the Board. Not only will you obtain great experience and resume fodder, you'll strengthen your relationship with the organization and its members in important ways.

As you can see, there are many ways to become more involved within the compliance community. Pick your top favorite way to give back, and start getting involved today!

Getting Sociable

I'm fascinated by the near total lack of comments on compliance-related pieces on the internet. The FCPA Blog, Compliance and Ethics Blog, articles posted on LinkedIn, pieces I've written on Compliance Kristy – if three comments are posted, the article must be controversial. I've seen articles with five thousand shares and zero comments. Why is it that in seemingly every corner of the internet, an active and vocal online community exists, where in compliance there is so little give and take?

I've asked this question to the community, and the answer that comes up again and again is this: fear. Compliance officers have jobs that lend themselves to secrecy. After all, it'd be crazy to write about your latest internal investigation on a public blog site. But as you the compliance officer are an adult (or at least pretending to be), with a little bit of common sense you can make a big difference in your visibility and profile while strengthening your name recognition and network.

Where do you start? Let's go with the usual suspects.

Facebook

While it's true that your dear Aunt Margaret probably isn't interested in the latest FCPA enforcement action, many groups exist on Facebook for the sharing of compliance-related information and ideas. Some of these groups, like the Society of Corporate Compliance and Ethics' group, are public, and anyone can join in the conversation or post material to the newsfeed. Here are some links to groups you might consider joining:

- SCCE: https://www.facebook.com/SCCE/
- Corporate Compliance Insights: https://www.facebook.com/CorporateComplianceInsights/
- Radical Compliance: https://www.facebook.com/radicalcompliance/

Twitter

Twitter is an unbeatable resource for the latest compliance-related news. It's also a fantastic place to get updates from thought leaders, and to meet and interact with them in real time. On Twitter, I've had conversations with everyone from reporters at the Wall Street Journal to contestants on the Bachelorette (guilty pleasure, don't judge).

Once you've started a Twitter account, you can search for individuals or companies that put out and share great content. I'd recommend you start with some or all of the following:

- Me: @KristyGrantHart
- Matt Kelly / Radical Compliance: @compliancememe
- Ben DiPietro / Wall Street Journal: @BenDiPietro1
- Michael Volkov: @mikevolkov20
- Richard Bistrong: @RichardBistrong

- Tom Fox: @GRCinfo
- FCPA Blog: @FCPA
- Jay Rosen: @FCPA_Monitor
- ETHIC Intelligence: @ETHICIntelligen
- EthiSphere: @ethisphere
- SCCE: @SCCE
- Roy Snell: @RoySnellSCCE
- Donna Boehme: @DonnaCBoehme
- Compliance Strategists: @CStrategists
- Gary Zack: @Gerry_Zack
- Robert Bond: @iionline
- Cordery Compliance: @CorderyUK

Once you've followed some compliance leaders, you're ready to participate in the conversation. If you don't want to add your own commentary – remember, Twitter is public, and tweets can be Googled – simply re-tweet articles or tweets you like or that provide good information.

I keep my Twitter account nearly entirely compliance-related, but some people choose to tweet about their personal lives or likes as well. It's up to you how much you share about yourself, but sharing material that will help the profession is definitely encouraged!

LinkedIn

It is hard for me to overstate how important LinkedIn has been for my career. I opened my LinkedIn account back when I was a litigator. It highlighted my skills and resume, but wasn't something I tended to actively. I didn't participate in groups or go through my newsfeed on a regular basis.

That changed in 2011 when I began searching for my first job in the corporate sector. All of a sudden, I noticed recruiters visiting my profile and sending me in-mails about potential jobs. I added a PDF of an article I wrote for Legal Week, and that immediately got me more attention and communications. By the time I moved into compliance, I'd updated my LinkedIn profile to be as strong as it could be.

My job as a CCO can be entirely credited to LinkedIn. To my surprise in 2013, I received an in-mail asking me if I was interested in applying for the CCO role at United International Pictures. LinkedIn brought me opportunities, and it can do the same for you.

Make sure you keep your profile up-to-date. Include a professional photo and keep your accomplishments front and center in your profile. Add information about the schools you attended and any professional activities or groups in which you participate. You never know when a fellow alumnus might contact you with an opportunity or a good connection.

LinkedIn can provide much more than an online resume-hosting service. Arguably its best feature is the Groups function, which allows sharing and conversation within a group of people with the same interests. There are several compliance-related groups that I would encourage you to consider joining, including:

- SCCE group: https://www.linkedin.com/groups/61769
- Anti-Corruption Experts:
  https://www.linkedin.com/groups/4852258
- IAPP Privacy Group:
  https://www.linkedin.com/groups/1243587

Once you've joined a group, be sure to post links to blog posts or articles that you find interesting and relevant. Your newsfeed can also be used for posting interesting articles. Be sure to steer away from anything overtly political, as this can be polarizing.

I'm still not convinced

If you're still not convinced about the value of social sharing, try lurking around the LinkedIn groups or on Twitter to see what people are sharing. Once you've watched for a while, try sharing something that you liked. You'll find out it isn't that scary. The benefits of participating in social media are enormous, and skipping out on the opportunity to show your knowledge and participate in the conversation doesn't make sense. Try it a couple of times – you'll probably like it!

Creating Your Personal Brand

You've probably heard the phrase "personal brand," but thought it only applied to hipsters and people in the marketing department. But here's the thing: you have a personal brand whether you're consciously creating it or not. A personal brand is frequently described as "what people think about you and how they'd describe you when you're not around." Your personal brand can encompass your major personality traits, the way you work, how you dress, what you're interested in and how you present yourself in public.

At a conference I attended recently, one wise compliance officer noted, "Cultivate your brand, because if you don't, people will do it for you."

> *Cultivate your brand, because if you don't,*
> *people will do it for you.*

People with strong personal brands quickly become more recognizable than those with weak brands. How does one create a personal brand? Whole books have been written on this subject, but I'm just going to cover the basics. Since people with strong personal brands are infrequent within the compliance profession, it's easy to stand out (in a good way!) if you consciously create one.

Signature Look

Several women in the compliance profession use jewelry to create a signature look, such as Former Chief Compliance Officer Marjorie Doyle, who is known for her large "statement" jewelry. During her keynote address at the SCCE conference in 2017, Ms. Doyle stated that she buys a piece of jewelry for every milestone event in her career.

Another highly prominent compliance officer wears colorful glasses that differentiate her and help her to stand out in a room. Yet another chooses colorful dresses with bright patterns to differentiate herself in a sea of black and blue suits.

Signature looks aren't limited to women's wear. One highly successful English data privacy lawyer always wears colorful patterned socks under his standard blue suit. Another wears smart pocket squares in his jackets, while a third wears beautiful ties.

I have bright red hair, which serves as a signature. And even though I live in London, where flats are required to manage the Tube and long walking distances between city blocks, I can always be found in high heels at work events. I'm originally from Los Angeles, and as everyone knows, you can take the girl out of California, but you can't take the California out of the girl. There is nothing inherently special about red hair or high heels, but the combination worn with consistency allows people to feel they know me and know what to expect from me when we meet.

Choose something to be your signature. Maybe you always dress sharply or with pizzazz? Maybe you're relentlessly casual – Silicon Valley's compliance officer look. Perhaps you only use colorful purses or bags, or always wear a string of pearls to events. Choosing a signature look will help you to stand out.

Your Signature Photo

Once you've chosen your signature piece, if possible, ensure that your headshot and/or social media picture includes it. If you're going for hipster sheik, ensure your LinkedIn profile shows your man-bun. If you've chosen the colorful glasses route, have them on in your profile picture for instant recognition.

The headshot you use should be consistent across all platforms. Let's say that you've got a LinkedIn profile, a Twitter account, a picture on your corporate website, and you're presenting at a conference next year. Ensure that the same photo is used for all of your social media accounts, as well as the corporate website and the conference brochure. You want to be instantly recognizable to those who know you or who are getting familiar with your name. Different pictures can create confusion and weaken your personal brand. By using one signature photo (which you should update at least every five years) across all platforms, you'll create a single brand image that will help with recognition and familiarity.

Other Signatures

It's not just clothing that can make up your personal brand. Public love of a sports team, a great affinity for animals – heck, even dancing can help you to stand out! Joe Murphy liked to dance so much that he started the Society of Dancing Compliance and Ethics Professionals. Everyone knows Joe will be the first person on the dance floor.

You can also choose a name and use it to describe yourself. Donna Boehme is described as, "the Lion of Compliance," a title she wears with pride. I sometimes joke that I'm a "Compliance

Kardashian" because I publish one-minute videos each week (the Wildly Effective Compliance Officer Tip of the Week) and do so much writing and media presenting. Maybe you're the Privacy Pro, or the Export Expert.

Brand Trust – Consistency is Key

One of the most important aspects of personal branding is consistency. Personal brands work best when they are consistent representations of your best self. Personal branding isn't just about outward appearance. It's also about how you choose to show up emotionally at work, what type of leader you choose to be, and how you manage your workload and co-workers. Are you a jolly or joyful person? Are you a strong and decisive leader? Are you a great team player who always chips in? Think about your top three qualities and list them here:

_____

_____

_____

Now create a sentence that incorporates one, two or all three of these qualities so that you can show them off. For instance, say that your top three qualities are: (1) usually cheerful, (2) a team player and (3) interested in others. Your brand promise might be, "Alan Richman is a cheerful team player who is interested in others."

Let's try another example. If your three top qualities are: (1) strategic leader, (2) thoughtful and (3) passionate about compliance, you'd end up with a brand promise like, "Zela Antoines is a thoughtful, strategic leader who is passionate about compliance."

Once you've developed your personal brand and signature look, be as consistent as possible so people know that they can trust your brand.

Case Study: Sue Gainor on Personal Branding

Sue Gainor is an incredible compliance pioneer. She's gone from the military to serving in the highest levels of government. She left and went into the corporate world, most recently as Vice President, Global Trade Controls, at the Boeing Company. Here, she talks about her personal brand.

"To me, a 'personal brand' is essentially a new term for reputation. It's how you want to be perceived in your professional environment. It's how you want your colleagues and associates to describe you to others. As such, your brand or reputation reflects both your values and your behaviors.

Over my 30+ year career, I've developed a reputation as a woman who's smart, friendly and personable, funny, outspoken, caring toward others, tough but fair, reliable, an advocate for women and minorities, and often a tad inappropriate in my humor. I've been described as someone who gets things done, thinks strategically, knows everyone, connects the dots, holds myself, others, and institutions to high standards, and acts with integrity. I'm willing to take risks and move positions both to learn and to advance. I have a finely tuned 'BS' meter and call people on it when I see it. When I'm wrong, I admit it and apologize for it. And sometimes my perfectionism gets in the way of getting things done.

When I was named Director of Defense Trade Controls Compliance at State Department in 2013, a media outlet quoted an unnamed source who described me as smart, having a strong policy background and military experience, and someone who 'doesn't take any guff.' When I read this description, I thought,

'I would be happy if that description is the epitaph on my tombstone!'"

Let's move from joining in and getting sociable outside of your organization, to joining in and collaborating with others inside your organization and beyond.

Chapter 10: Collaboration is Key! Playing Well with Others

"The problem is not the problem. The problem is your attitude about the problem."
– Captain Jack Sparrow

In compliance, I've often felt like the new kid in the corporate playground. Everyone already has their friends. They know their role and their routine, then here comes compliance to mess things up. Turf wars erupt, gossip begins to fly, people choose sides, and all of a sudden, this new role seems to have more headaches than breakthroughs.

In many companies, you will be the first compliance officer they've ever had. "What is compliance anyway? Why do we need you?" In others, you'll come into a place where roles aren't properly defined, and you'll have to scramble to try to make friends and win influence.

There are functions that nearly every compliance professional deals with in larger companies. These functions include Legal, Human Resources, Audit and Procurement. Turf wars erupt and escalate when roles and responsibilities aren't properly defined. I've seen these relationships sour, but I've also seen many thrive when forward thinking is employed. How do we work in a Wildly Successful way with other functions?

Four Wildly Successful Ways to Work with Human Resources

HR was here first, and they know it. Human Resources personnel handle salaries, hiring, firing and discipline at most companies, and they tend not to appreciate compliance stepping on their toes. You can try to defuse the turf war with the following techniques.

Define Roles and Responsibilities for Internal Investigations

Turf wars seem to develop out of nowhere during internal investigations. In the ugliest scenarios, HR and Compliance hide information from each other or perform investigations in silos, occasionally duplicating each other's work. To avoid this from happening, it is best to define your roles and responsibilities for internal investigations before you engage in them. Meet to agree on where to keep documents, what templates will be used, and how to determine who will take the lead on the internal investigations at the outset so you don't run into problems later.

What if you've never developed a protocol for internal investigations, or tensions are already running high? No problem – set up a meeting with HR to ask them how they think internal investigations should work. By engaging them in the conversation, you can begin to build a rapport to make decisions together.

Agree on How to Share Exit Interview Data

I've worked with a number of compliance departments that never see the data from exit interviews. Not only is this information critical for taking the temperature of the culture in the company, this data can provide invaluable assistance for understanding risk in the organization. Compliance will see exit interview data through a different lens than HR. Where HR might simply see bullying by a manager, compliance may see potential fraud, cover-ups, conflicts of interest, or broader culture issues, which could indicate ethical failure by the manager.

Agree on how you will share exit interview data. Perhaps there are data privacy concerns, so you can get an anonymized version of the data? Maybe you can get a monthly report amalgamating the results? Perhaps HR can add you as a database user so you're able to access the data without their direct involvement? Exit interview data is key, and you need to have access to it to do the best job you can in your role.

Agree on How to Handle the Separation of Issues

In most companies HR reviews HR issues, but it isn't always clear where HR issues end and compliance issues begin. For instance, when a conflict of interest involves a romantic relationship between two co-workers, is that an HR issue or a compliance issue? What about a situation where a report of wage and hour violations includes a retaliation compliant (a violation of the Code of Conduct)?

Agreeing on the separation of issues beforehand will avoid problems when a large issue arises. Try to set up a protocol for determining which issue is the foremost issue, if more than one issue is present or overlap occurs. By agreeing early, you'll stop problems from occurring later.

Create a Close-Out Protocol for Whistle-Blower Complaints Relating to HR Issues (which are most of them!)

How many calls to your whistle-blower hotline relate to HR issues? All of them? If your company is like most, nearly all of the calls received by the whistle-blower hotline relate to HR issues. From reports of someone smoking in the bathroom to commonplace, I-hate-my-manager calls, the majority of whistle-blower complaints come in regarding HR issues.

If you've developed protocols for dealing with these issues, the next step is ensure that you receive information on the disposition of these investigations. You should be able to establish that these whistle-blower complaints were properly investigated and closed-out. Ideally, you'd have access to the final reports to ensure the investigation was handled correctly, but at the very least, you need the ability to verify that the investigation was completed and the case closed.

Four Wildly Successful Ways to Work with Legal

The Legal Department can be your best friend or your worst enemy. Many of the duties that fall within the compliance remit overlap with traditional legal work. In addition, many compliance departments have the additional challenge of being situated within the Legal Department, or of being overseen by the General Counsel instead of an independent CCO. What can you do to make this relationship easier?

Carefully Delineate Your Responsibilities

You've just received notice of a potential competition violation or a data breach. Who is in charge, Compliance or Legal? Deciding these types of questions before they become an issue can be incredibly helpful. In one company in which I worked, if there was a regulatory investigation or an outside competition inquiry, the Legal Department handled it. If there was an internal competition complaint or concern, Compliance handled it. This delineation allowed for the easy assignment of tasks when an issue came up.

One company I work with separates contract processing as follows: Legal is primarily in charge of contract drafting, negotiation and review; and Compliance handles any anti-bribery, modern slavery or sanctions-related clauses, as well as any supplier codes of conduct. Legal relies on approval from Compliance for these specific clauses and supplier code reviews, and Compliance doesn't interfere with the rest of the contracting process.

Talk to Legal about all of the areas they handle. If your company's Compliance Department is new, there may be reluctance by the Legal Department to hand off responsibility. After all, Legal has almost certainly been entirely in charge of legal and compliance issues before Compliance came to the company. Try to be understanding but firm in creating delineated responsibilities so that you can work together effectively.

Seek Out Legal's Advice and Ask for Help

I've been a lawyer for over a decade, and one thing I know for sure is that almost all lawyers like to feel respected and valued for their wisdom and knowledge. If you have questions or simply want a second opinion, make a habit of consulting the Legal Department. By coming to them for advice, counsel or a second opinion, you'll be showing them respect and appreciation. Legal is much more likely to respect your position if you show them you respect theirs.

One of my consulting clients was looking to proactively formalize a plan for data breach response. It was decided Compliance would decide when and how to notify regulators and customers if there were a breach, and Legal would perform the contract review to determine contractual obligations. For instance, if four individuals from three corporate customers were affected by a breach, the lawyers in Legal would review the contracts to determine whether there was a specific timeframe within which each company needed to be notified. Compliance would report the breach to the individuals who were affected.

Asking for help is important, but it must be done judiciously, especially if your Legal department is busy. Be careful, but ask for help when you need it.

Acknowledge the Trouble that Can Occur if You're an Attorney

If you are a practicing attorney, understand that for many in the Legal Department, there will be confusion about what you do in Compliance. Does your work invoke privilege? Sometimes but not always? Why is it your job to protect the company by building an ethical culture and considering what's right, when the Legal Department's mandate is to help the company find the lines of what it can get away with? Attorneys may feel threatened or not understand how Compliance is different from Legal. Acknowledge and anticipate this disconnect so that you can work to educate your counter-parts.

Acknowledge the Trouble that Can Occur if You're not an Attorney

If you're not a practicing attorney, understand that the lawyers in the Legal Department may not understand why you've been given such a broad mandate over important work without the ability to invoke privilege directly, or to concern yourself with the law in the same way the lawyers do. Acknowledge and anticipate this issue and show the Legal team that you're willing to seek their assistance and advice with respect to tricky issues and problems that might need to be dealt with under privilege.

Four Wildly Successful Ways to Work with Internal Audit

In many companies, Internal Auditors know more than you do about the everyday life of the business. You may do training on the ground for one or two days, but Internal Audit stays for one to two weeks or more.

Outposts in Sudan? Small business units that never reach critical mass in order for you to travel to them? Travel ban for compliance or other training? Internal Audit probably still visits in person. How can you leverage this tremendous resource in a way that is palatable to Internal Audit and helpful to the compliance program?

In some companies there is a turf war between Internal Audit and Compliance, but there's no reason for that. Used properly, Internal Audit can be your best friend. You can help each other to do your jobs more effectively. Here are four highly effective ways to work with Internal Audit.

Institute a Pre-Audit Check-In

Before I began Spark Compliance Consulting, I was Chief Compliance Officer at United International Pictures, the joint venture of Paramount Pictures and Universal Pictures for movie distribution in 65 countries. Although I traveled to an average of 16 countries each year to do in-person compliance training, I could never visit all of the countries. However, our Internal Audit team did. I asked our head of Internal Audit to have a pre-audit phone call with me whenever he went to a new country. On our call we would discuss the following:

- Are there any known compliance issues in the country?
- Are there any regulatory investigations going on, or hot laws in the country to which we're responding?
- Has anyone in the territory declared a conflict of interest that we want to follow up on? If so, is there anything Internal Audit should be reviewing while they are there?

This check-in allowed Internal Audit to be highly aware of any issues. Of course, there were times I couldn't share information about an investigation or an unresolved conflict of interest, but when I could, it was extremely helpful, as Internal Audit would keep their eyes open when they were visiting to spot problems they might not otherwise see.

Add Compliance Elements to the Audit Scope

One way you can work with Internal Audit is to add a couple of compliance-related elements to the audit scope. You may need to negotiate with Internal Audit or the finance leaders to do this, but it is well worth the investment. Consider adding these compliance elements to the audit scope:

High-Risk Receipts: Request that Internal Auditors evaluate one or two randomly selected high-risk receipts. If your company uses consultants in countries with a high-risk for bribery, instruct Internal Audit to review one or two invoices from these consultants to look for red flags. Or, if your company imports or exports materials, have Internal Audit review several customs invoices and receipts looking for miscellaneous fees or facilitation payments. These checks on high-risk receipts can effectively help you find problems.

Third-Parties: In many companies, Internal Audit may visit important third-party suppliers or business partners on the ground. In these cases, have Internal Audit ask the third-party about its compliance and ethics program. Internal Audit doesn't need to comment or instruct about such programs; they can simply report back on whether the intermediary has a formal compliance program or Code of Conduct. This information can help you to prioritize your resources to focus on higher-risk intermediaries that don't have their own internal resources for handling ethics and compliance issues.

Expense Reports: Ask Internal Audit to do a spot-check of expense reports or receipts for gifts and entertainment to see if your gifts and entertainment policies are being followed. Internal Audit should try to find receipts for gifts or entertainment offered to government officials if they are available, but either way, a spot-check of such receipts or expense reports can prove invaluable when assessing compliance with your procedures and policies.

Materials: Request that Internal Auditors check to see that compliance materials are available and posted where you've instructed. For instance, if you have posters for your Ethics Helpline, Internal Audit's scope can include a check to verify that the poster is up in the local language and readily visible to all employees. This is an easy way to ensure that your instructions are being followed globally.

Have a Post-Audit Catch-Up

After the audit is complete, have Internal Audit call you for an informal catch-up. Ask about the culture in the country or business unit. Were the salespeople stressed out or under unreasonable sales goals that might lead them to compromise their ethics? Is there a dictatorial style of management or bullying occurring? How was morale?

Recently, the Institute of Business Ethics published a fascinating white paper on the capacity of Internal Audit to perform checks on culture. I attended the launch party for the paper in London, and much of the discussion revolved around the observation that many Internal Auditors are uncomfortable trying to quantify culture in a way that could confidently be included in an audit report. My suggestion is that you bridge this reality by giving Internal Audit space to informally report to you about the culture they see during their audits so that you can follow up where appropriate, and target training or travel to countries and business units that may have problems or issues.

Do Audit-Specific Training

In order to best utilize the Internal Audit team, you should arrange special live or webinar training to help Internal Auditors identify the red flags they are likely to see during their audits. Instead of performing generic anti-bribery training, talk to the Internal Audit team about red flags, and give them real examples of how other companies have gotten in trouble or share examples of problematic payments you've found at your company. The more information Internal Audit has, the better. My experience is that good Internal Auditors enjoy the hunt for improper payments, and arming them with specific indicators is a fun experience that you will both enjoy.

Internal Audit can be your best friend. The men and women in these roles spend more time on the ground than you ever will, unless you're performing an investigation. You can leverage their time to enhance your program and create a stronger defense against illegal and unethical behavior.

Four Wildly Successful Ways to Work with Procurement

Procurement is becoming a more critical friend to Compliance. As regulations regarding modern slavery and human rights abuses come to the forefront, Procurement is in a unique position to help you to manage these big risks. They can also help you with anti-trust/competition concerns and anti-bribery due diligence. To ensure you get the best out of Procurement, you should...

Train Procurement on Red Flags for Modern Slavery

Procurement is in a great spot to catch signs of modern slavery, human trafficking and human rights abuses. If a price is too good to be true, it probably is, and may be available on the backs of people forced into labor or indentured servitude. In addition to spotting totally unrealistic low prices, Procurement should be trained about other red flags, like a refusal to enter into audit clauses that allow for on-site visits in high-risk countries. The more information Procurement is given, the more likely they are to see red flags so they can warn Compliance when there might be a problem.

Ensure They Understand Competition Issues and Price-Sharing Issues

I can't tell you the number of companies I've gone into where someone in Procurement or Purchasing has bragged that they got a great price by sending one vendor's quote to a competitor, then asking the competitor to match or beat the quote. Instead of discussing the company's needs and asking for the best possible price, Procurement accidentally engages itself in conduct that could be considered anti-competitive and that could get the company in trouble.

Be sure to train the Procurement department on competition/anti-trust issues so that you're sure they won't accidentally engage in anti-competitive behavior.

Have a Clear Conflict of Interest Process with Procurement

Sure, you've got the annual disclosure you require from your employees or managers to discover conflicts of interest, but is it enough? One place Procurement can be infinitely helpful is in including a conflicts of interest disclosure on the part of vendors and suppliers as part of your on-boarding process. A simple check box or two-sentence section within on-boarding forms can make an enormous difference. An example would be, "Please check the box if any of your relatives work at our Company." If a vendor clicks "Yes," Compliance can follow up to ensure that no conflict of interest exists.

By asking Procurement to help you root out conflicts of interest from the third-party providers, you'll get a more fulsome picture of the risks facing the company from unfair business practices.

Make ONE Due Diligence Questionnaire to Include in the Review Process

Vendors and suppliers complain bitterly about the multitude of questionnaires and forms they have to fill out in order to work with many large companies. Bribery due diligence? Please fill out this online form. And after you finish that, fill out the data privacy questionnaire, then the human rights and modern slavery survey. Perhaps you finish off with the health and safety questionnaire, as well as the diversity form.

Instead of requiring multiple due diligence instruments, work with Procurement to come up with a single form that can be filled out by potential vendors and suppliers. Procurement should notify compliance (or the relevant department) if it gets a concerning answer. By having one streamlined process, you'll make it easier for everyone.

Dealing Effectively with Management

There are many important techniques for dealing with management – so many that they belong in another book (see

How to Be a Wildly Effective Compliance Officer for in-depth information on using motivation, persuasion and influence to become an in-demand business asset). The most important thing you can do with management is to understand what they want so you can be a strategic partner who helps them to get it. The more they trust that you're on their team, the more likely you are to be influential.

Collaborating as a Committee

Some people swear by Compliance Committees and Compliance Liaison networks. Bringing together representatives from each of the functions listed above can mean information exchanges hands easily and all at once. People can learn from each other. These types of groups need strong leadership and well-thought-out agendas so they don't meander into "yet another useless meeting."

If you decide to start a Compliance Committee, be careful to craft the meeting as a place where things get done. Assign people tasks so that they know what they need to do to help the compliance program. Meetings where you simply talk about what you've done aren't useful and won't engender success. Instead of saying, "Last month, we launched our new Code of Conduct and associated training," try, "We've launched our Code of Conduct, and we need each of you to discuss it with your team using the management cascade slides we've distributed. Please report back to me within two weeks so I can track which teams have been taught."

Can't we just all get along?

The most important skill in working with the other functions is to properly define your role and theirs before an issue arises. If it's too late for that, start now. Listen to what the other function thinks and wants, then try to come to a written set of rules defining your relationship and responsibilities.

Strategic Friends and Allies

Compliance can feel like an awfully lonely profession, especially if you're the lone practitioner in your office. But take heart! It doesn't have to be that way. When you have strategic friends and allies, you can make the most of your place in the profession.

Strategic Use of Trade Associations and Conferences

We've already covered the benefits of joining a trade association like the SCCE or the Ethics and Compliance Initiative. You meet like-minded people and have the capacity to learn what other companies are doing. But strategic use of conferences is different than merely joining an organization. If you plan your conference attendance correctly, it can make a world of difference to your career.

If you're thinking you don't have time to attend a conference because you're too busy with work, think again. It's easy to tell ourselves we can't get to a conference this time. After all, there's the time lost to travel to the conference, the cost, weeks awaiting reimbursement and the never-ending ding of the mobile device letting you know that while you're in sessions, people at your organization still need you to be doing your compliance work. But while it may seem best to skip conference attendance, you shouldn't. Here's why.

Creating Your Network Before You Need It

The time to build a network is before you need it. You've no doubt known someone who looked totally secure in her job, who finds out with zero notice that her company is closing, or having layoffs that include her. Suddenly she is scrambling to find another position. You can use conferences to build your network before something like that happens to you.

The Best Time to Build a Network is Before You Need It

About a month ago I got a call from a former colleague of mine. After 15 years in the same blue-chip company, the compliance function was moved to an office in another state, and he wasn't invited to go. He was devastated. He'd seen an ad for a job he was interested in, and he noted that I was connected to the hiring manager via LinkedIn. Could I offer an introduction? You bet I could.

The reason I could help him was because I'd met the hiring manager at a conference three years earlier. We'd kept in touch, and I was able to put them in contact and send his resume along. Guess what? He got the job. The truth is, the best jobs are almost always filled by people who come with a recommendation from a trusted source. By attending conferences you build your network now, before you need it.

If you find yourself downsized or your company goes out of business, there's nothing like a vibrant network to help you find your next role. Alternatively, if you've outgrown your current job, your network can be your eyes and ears to get you that promotion you so richly deserve.

The best time to build a network is before you need it.

Use Conferences to Learn Best Practices

Your manager has probably asked upon occasion, "Well, what are other companies doing?" This vexing question is asked throughout the world when compliance officers meet with management to discuss new laws. Whether it's the European General Data Protection Regulation, dealing effectively with harassment, or the UK Modern Slavery Act, people at your company not only expect you to know the law, they also expect you to know what to do about complying with it. Conferences are fantastic places to learn what other companies are doing in response to the same challenges you're facing.

We're lucky in compliance in that we're able to share our work strategies with each other without fear of anti-trust violations. The ability to take advantage of other people's knowledge is one of the best things about conference attendance.

Strategic Use of Outside Counsel

Outside counsel can be a great ally. Law firms routinely put out information about new laws, court cases, regulatory enforcement actions and trends going through the industry. Get yourself on the mailing list of the best law firms in your town. Frequently all it takes is going to their website to sign up, or calling reception and asking to be added to their email blasts.

Law firms also frequently offer free webinars and meetings where you can receive continuing education credit if you're a lawyer. CEI credits, which contribute to your ongoing CCEP or CCEP-I status, can often be obtained as well.

Finally, if your company gets into trouble, or you need immediate help with an internal investigation or regulatory action, it's great to have someone trusted to turn to. Developing the relationship between your company and outside counsel before you need it can make it much easier if the worst happens.

Strategic Use of Consulting Firms

Consulting firms can provide invaluable insight and help with structuring or improving your compliance program.

Consulting companies range in size from the Big 4 (Deloitte, KPMG, PwC, EY) to solopreneurs.

Experienced consultants can make your job easier. If you need to do a risk assessment, they can complete it in two months, as opposed to the six months to a year you'd need to do it. They can also give you plans to complete difficult projects. For instance, my company, Spark Compliance Consulting, has been creating GDPR readiness plans for many multi-national companies. The companies know they need to comply with GDPR, but they don't know how to do it. We provide a strategic, pragmatic road map, along with templates and explanations about how to use them. The compliance officer can then do the implementation, which is infinitely easier with a pre-created plan.

Lastly, never underestimate the power of a good compliance program evaluation or assessment. Program evaluations provide concrete evidence of the effectiveness of all the areas of your program. Consulting companies will know best practices, because they deal with many different companies. They can provide crucial recommendations to make your program better. Also, management may listen to an outside firm more than they listen to you. Program evaluations keep your program strong.

Strategic Use of Technology Vendors and Support Services

At conferences, many people avoid eye contact with the vendors in the exhibition hall, or try not to engage with them. Frequently this happens because you already know you don't have the budget for whatever they're selling. Rather than avoiding eye contact, the next time you're in the exhibit hall, speak to each of the vendors that has a product you might use in the future. Why?

First, when you see new technology or a vendor offering a service that can make your job easier or more efficient, you can take this information back with you to make a case for the service within your company.

Second, if you get budget the following year or join a new company, you can advocate for the technology or service. If you don't talk to the vendors, you don't know the help they can offer.

Third, vendors often have cutting-edge information about the new trends in compliance. Because they speak to and serve so many companies, they can help you to stay on top of what is happening.

Strategic Use of Recruiters

In addition to networking with other compliance professionals, try to befriend a recruiter specializing in compliance. You can look for one in your town or city, or engage one of the international recruiting agencies focusing on the placement of lawyers and other risk-related executives.

You can sign up to receive the recruiting company's newsletter, or put a note in your calendar to check in with the recruiter once every six months or so to see what is happening in your part of the compliance industry. This way, not only do you keep on top of hiring trends, but also if you ever need to look for another job, you have someone you know who you can call.

Case Study: Rob Baron on Recruiting for Compliance Roles

Rob Baron is a Director at Baron Crawford, an international legal and compliance search/recruiting company based in London. I caught up with Rob to find out how compliance officers can best position themselves for success when they're searching for a job.

Kristy: What are the critical skills employers are looking for in compliance professionals?

Rob: An understanding of laws and regulations is important, but knowing how the laws and regulations are applied – and how they can practically be implemented in a commercial environment – is more important.

Most companies are looking for an approachable face for compliance – a person who balances risk with the commercial realities to help facilitate their business. They also are looking for a deep-thinking and strong communicator who can effectively promote a message in different ways to different audiences. In essence, companies are looking for:

- Knowledge
- Commercial awareness
- Strong communication abilities, and
- A strategic and operational approach to compliance

Kristy: How do you recommend compliance officers work with recruiters if they are looking for a job?

Rob: I would recommend the compliance officer makes sure they are in contact with recruiters who have a strong presence in the compliance area and the sector they are interested in. Compliance officers should also remember that no one recruiting company will be able to represent them for all the roles in the market.

It seems obvious, but compliance officers should always try to meet with a recruiter in person. The recruiter can do a much better job of promoting the candidate if they have met them face-to-face.

Kristy: How can compliance officers start preparing for their next role, even if they're happy at their current job?

Rob: I recommend making sure your information on sites such as LinkedIn is always up to date, so employers and recruiters know exactly what you are currently doing. Self-promotion by presenting at conferences can also be useful in extending your visibility. I recommend building your network as strongly as possible. Often your next role will originate from someone you have met or who recommends you to someone else.

I would also think about what you need to do to get to the next level, whether that is trying to get more management experience, leading projects in your current role, or taking a course that adds to your overall experience and appeal.

Kristy: What advice do you give compliance officers applying for jobs?

Rob: Approach a job search systematically, taking note of which jobs you have applied to and when. I advocate being proactive with any application. As I said previously, meeting personally with a recruiter gives you a much better chance of being successful. Always enquire about roles you are interested in with your recruiter, because a recruiter may not automatically think of you, even if it might be a good fit.

When applying directly to jobs without any interaction with a recruiter, I would always recommend sending a short cover note that explains why you are applying. Your note should highlight your strengths and deal with any obvious reasons why a company might not consider you. If you do not hear back when applying for a role, I would also advise trying to follow up with HR or a manager.

Kristy: What are the trends and hot areas in compliance, and what skills should compliance officers develop in response?

Rob: Most recently, privacy has been a major area of focus for obvious reasons. Even though many compliance roles are kept separate from privacy, having knowledge of the area can be very beneficial.

We have seen a growing trend for the use of technology and tools, including artificial intelligence. That is only going to increase. At the same time, the set up and management of compliance structures remains the key area of interest and development.

Chapter 11: The Future of Compliance

I'm often asked to look into my crystal ball to talk about the future of the compliance profession. Compliance is still in its infancy. We have yet to see what happens when we are fully accepted as a profession separate from legal and sustainability.

Following are three people's ideas about the future of compliance. Some of them are controversial, but each provides a strong point of view to consider.

Case Study:
Hugh Bigwood on the Future of Compliance

Hugh Bigwood is a pioneer in the world of compliance. He's the Global Head of Compliance at one of the world's leading mining companies, as well as a former compliance officer in the pharmaceutical field.

Here, Hugh answers questions on the use of behavioral economics, why he calls his compliance team "sales and marketing," and the future of compliance.

Kristy: You're a big fan of behavioral economics as it relates to compliance. What do you mean by behavioral economics, and how can a compliance officer use behavioral economics to be Wildly Successful?

Hugh: Every day we are constantly making decisions. Behavioral economics, behavioral science, or nudge theory helps us model that behavior, understand the influences, and ultimately predict behavior. None of this is new. Consumer sales and marketing have been doing this for years.

Most compliance issues can be traced back to an individual making a decision at a single point in time. It's often in the heat of the moment. We need to take into account all of the influencers in that moment. Our compliance role is to remain an influencer in the choice made by that individual. The future of compliance is where we can start to predict who will make those decisions, where those decisions will take place and what the decision is likely to be.

There are many decision models out there, but largely the decision-making process will have four components:

1. Opportunity
2. Capability
3. Motivation
4. Rationalization

The interesting thing is that if we can alter or intervene in just one of these four, we can change or influence the decision made. What we haven't seen are these approaches being consciously used in the compliance area.

Kristy: Can you give me some examples of how behavioral economics can be applied in compliance?

Hugh: We know from research studies that if someone is reminded of their obligations under a code of conduct just before an activity, they are more likely to act in accordance with that code. Trade association meetings are a known opportunity for antitrust risks. We generally know when these meetings will be held, and who will attend. What if we texted or emailed our anti-trust advice to people attending these trade association meetings just before the meeting? The cost of the intervention is low, but the likelihood that people will remember the rules is higher when they are reminded, so this should reduce overall risk.

There is a great story presented by Robert Cialdini and Steve J. Martin in their book, *Yes! 50 Secrets from the Science of Persuasion*. If a waiter/waitress leaves a mint with your bill, the tip will be around 3%. If the waiter/waitress leaves two mints, the tip doesn't double – it goes up to 14%. However, if the waiter/waitress leaves one mint, walks away, stops, turns back and says, "Just for you, have another mint," the tip will increase by a whopping 23%.

This is one of my favorite stories, as it shows that people's behavior can be influenced significantly by something as simple as a mint. It shows the impact made when things are made personal to an individual.

So what can we learn from this for our compliance programs? Well, what if online training gave people a choice of which class to take? Even better, what if the person was asked a few questions before the training started, so they felt that the training was chosen specifically for them? What if the system recognized the person logging on, and started the questions using their name? What if there was a reward for early completion? What if the participant could pass a test before taking the training, so they never had to do the training in the first place?

The cost of the intervention is low, but the likelihood that people will remember the rules is higher when they are reminded, so reminding them should reduce overall risk.

It has been shown that if people know others have acted in a certain way, they are more likely to follow suit. Use of hotlines and whistle-blowing is not yet an accepted societal norm in many places. What if we ran a campaign that advertised the number of reports received and the incidents the reports helped to prevent? Will this make people feel more comfortable about reporting? What if we went one step further and gave the hotline a personality, so people felt they were talking to a real person, rather than accessing a system or process?

These are all things I have tried, and all have showed a beneficial outcome.

Kristy: You call your compliance team "sales and marketing." Can you tell me about that?

Hugh: I have to sell people on the idea of compliance. It's our product. People at the company need to buy in, and the more they buy in, the more likely they will think and consider how they act. With that concept in mind I have structured my group as follows.

The Sales Force – the Compliance group: The compliance group is the sales force. It consists of the regionally based compliance managers, who are the main face of compliance.

We need to know our customers (the business). We need to study their likes and dislikes, their business operations and the environment they are operating in. We need to sell the "product." We need to be out with the business at all levels creating discussion, providing guidance etc.

Depending on the customer and the risks that they face, we may have to adjust the product, and give it a new color or extra accessories, as each customer may not like exactly the same version of our product. It may not fit their particular environment or risks.

Research, Development, and Manufacturing – the Compliance Operations Group: The Operations Group does research and development, as well as manufacturing. This group works to plan ahead – where is the market going, where are the new risks, what will be the next trend? Can we predict where we need to devote and direct resource?

Products are never stationary; they always develop over time. We need to develop our product – bring out version 2.0, version 3.0, etc. We need to provide the systems to support our "product," to support the Compliance Managers, the Investigators, and also the businesses. We need to take feedback from the sales force about how things are developing, where the overlaps are, and how we can make things more effective and more efficient.

After-sales Service – the Investigations Group: The Investigations Group is best described as part of customer support and after-sales service. This group needs to deal with issues when they arise, and look into them to see what has gone wrong, to help prevent reoccurrences. This feedback is essential not only to the sales force, but also to research, development and manufacturing.

It should also be remembered that how a company deals with complaints has a huge impact on how the overall product is seen. That means the customer experience is critical. The customer has to feel that they have been listened to, and, although they may not like the results, that they have been treated fairly and understand the outcome.

Sales can't operate without a product to sell. The best product can be ruined by bad selling, and a great salesman doesn't make a bad product good. Bad after-sales service can kill all future sales regardless of how well we sell and how great the product is. We are all linked and need to work together.

It is key for me that there is a common understanding of the approach. The group must be aligned in what their respective roles are and what it is trying to achieve. This is not a common approach for most compliance programs. But given that no one has invented the perfect compliance program, and no one has got the metrics to prove effectiveness – this is where I believe we need to go.

Kristy: What advice would you give someone going into compliance about building a successful career?

Hugh: I fell into compliance by accident. I was working as an in-house lawyer, and my general counsel, at the time, came to me saying that since I was so critical of the compliance group, perhaps I should take over running part of it? After the first year, I knew I would never go back to being a pure lawyer.

Compliance is not an easy role. You are not always welcomed. Some of the decisions you may have to make will not be popular, and you will often be seen as the "bad guy." You'll be blamed for everything (even for things you have never done or said). You need to build quite a thick skin, and there is no doubt you will need to be courageous at some point in your career.

One of my first-ever managers told me good lawyers follow precedent, but great lawyers make their own. That approach has stayed with me through my career and applies to compliance as much as the law.

Never be afraid to try different approaches. Just because something hasn't been tried in the area of Compliance doesn't mean it won't work – play, experiment, don't just follow the crowd. Be willing to fail so you can learn.

Don't laboriously follow the decisions of DOJ/SEC settlements or deferred prosecution agreements in the UK, as if these are going to really show you what an effective program will look like. You have to remember that these are reactions to something that has already gone wrong. The aim of a compliance program has to be preventing things going wrong in the first place.

I often joke that I think people come out of their houses in the morning and are hit by a bolt of lightning that switches off half their brains. People often behave differently at work, leaving behind common sense, doing things that they would never dream of doing if it were their own money or their own property. To be a successful compliance manager, use your whole brain.

Kristy: What characteristics do you look for when you're hiring a compliance officer to join your team?

Hugh: I have a fairly diverse team. I have no preference for a particular background, and currently have people with finance backgrounds, procurement backgrounds, one or two newly-graduated former students, some IT backgrounds, a few ex-police officers, and the odd lawyer. Their educational backgrounds range from criminology to genetics. What perhaps I am missing now is someone with a marketing and sales background. The audience I am working with is far from uniform, so I really value the diversity different backgrounds create. I am selling a product, so my team needs to reflect the diversity of the customer.

People often ask whether experience in a particular industry is important. Business or commercial experience is important, but again I am not worried about the particular industry – each sector has some unique attributes, but generally there are more commonalities than differences.

I have worked in multiple sectors. I started as a taxi driver and have since worked in pharma, medical devices, fish farming, agribiotech, infant formula, the food industry, and now in mining. Every industry has brought me something new but also has reinforced the similarities.

Regardless of background, there are a few key characteristics I look for:

- *Impeccable integrity:* I'm afraid I am a bit of a Puritan. If you are going to sell a product involving integrity, then you have to reflect it yourself. I am sometimes amazed by how many invites I get from suppliers to come to networking meetings at the back of a top restaurant. How will it look if I am trying to educate a manager on the evils of accepting entertainment while I am doing the same?

- *Good communication skills:* Good storytellers make great compliance managers as they can engage the audience.

- *Good business experience*: We have to know how the business operates. There can't be any ivory towers.

- *Pragmatic:* Perfection is rarely possible.

If I am hiring, I want the candidate to make me think, to bring something new, to teach me – you are never too old to learn and, despite what we may like to think, bosses don't know it all.

Kristy: Where do you see the future of compliance going?

Hugh: That's a difficult one. Ultimately, why do we have compliance groups? A really successful compliance manager is one whose aim must be to make his role ultimately redundant. Luckily, for those of us that have made this area our career, I think this may still be a long way off!

For the future, I think the following:

- There will be a greater focus on ethics and culture, as opposed to policing a set of rules.

- Behavioral prediction will be used more and more. OK – *Minority Report* may be a step too far, but how far could we go?

- The compliance profession will take a greater role in influencing new legislation, not just reacting to it.

Case Study: Lisa Beth Lentini on Mindfulness and Gratitude

Lisa Beth Lentini, JD/MBA, LLM, is one of my favorite people. She was my first boss in the compliance world, and it is not an overestimation to say that without her, I wouldn't be where I am now. She offered to answer my questions about the future of compliance with respect to mindfulness and gratitude.

Kristy: You recently completed a business class on mindfulness and gratitude. Can you tell us about it?

Lisa Beth: As part of my own personal development journey, I had the great fortune to enroll in a mindfulness half-day retreat. I had always enjoyed doing little meditations to center myself from time to time, but had never really dedicated any time to the study. Halfway into the retreat at the University of Minnesota Center for Spirituality and Healing, I was hooked and knew that mindfulness was essential to a healthy compliance team.

It wasn't long after my own retreat that I was able to make the business case for the senior leaders on my compliance team to schedule time for an eight-week course on mindfulness at work. The compliance profession in general has a high burn-out rate, due in no small part to the stress associated with the job. My goal in the mindfulness at work plan was to equip each of the leaders with new techniques and tools to live as healthy a work life as possible.

I believe mindful leaders create healthier teams and healthier teams do better, more thoughtful work. All of this leads to greater productivity and much better relationships both within and outside the department. Having a healthy mind leads to a happier workplace.

Kristy: You've found a unique way for you and your team to show gratitude to people in the business. What did you do, and what was the response?

Lisa Beth: Gratitude is a foundational component for a happy life. It isn't enough to go through your day in a mindless and self-involved fashion. What really makes life beautiful are the connections and relationships built. We were inspired as part of this process by a great video by SoulPancake called *"The Happiness Project."*

As part of our own efforts to be more mindful, we have put gratitude at the center. We do this in a couple of ways:

- We make time at every meeting to recognize successes in each other and thank members of the team for their efforts and support.
- We have a gratitude jar to fill with memories of all the things we are grateful for.
- We developed a branded card for the team that we use to express gratitude to our internal clients.

The branded card has been a huge success with our internal clients. Many of them have actually framed the cards or displayed them in their offices. There is even one person who said he hadn't received such a thoughtful and beautifully drafted thank you in the forty years he had spent with the company.

The bottom line for me is gratitude is good for the person receiving thanks, but it is just as good for the person who is genuinely providing the thanks. Everyone benefits, and it starts a beautiful, virtuous cycle of positivity that reaps long-term benefits. A client who feels gratitude thinks twice before responding negatively to a compliance request. Gratitude humanizes our profession and allows us to be a positive change in the world.

Kristy: Do you use mindfulness outside of your work life? If so, how - and how does it make your life better?

Lisa Beth: Every day, I try to use mindfulness. Some days are clearly more successful than others – just like in exercise when some workouts are easier or better than others. Mindfulness is a continuous practice and needs to be incorporated into all elements of life in order to truly have the desired impact.

I often find that mindfulness helps me to be present in conversations with others in this increasingly distracted/distracting world. With technology and communication increasing the pace of life, taking a moment to re-center and move from a reactive/defensive state to a productive/towards state of mind helps everyone and leads to better engagement and interactions.

Kristy: Do you think more businesses and compliance leaders should use mindfulness and gratitude? If so, how can they start?

Lisa Beth: The best business and compliance leaders incorporate mindfulness and gratitude into everyday interactions. They know that the heart and soul of any place is the people, and the only way to truly honor a person is to "see" them, recognize them, and be grateful that they choose to be engaged every day. Mindful leaders are leaders with principles who place people first as the keys to not only the company's success but the leader's success as well.

I think the best place to start is to take some time to get grounded. Try meditation for just a minute or two. There are plenty of apps and resources that are available to give just a quick start and overview of the practice.

Make a choice to learn more about how mindfulness can benefit you personally and professionally. Learn the neuroscience behind how mindfulness benefits organizations. Once you have a started with the practice, you will find your own path to incorporating a form of mindfulness that works for you.

Case Study: Ricardo Pellafone on the Future of Training and Communications

Ricardo Pellafone is the brilliant creator and founder of Broadcat, a specialist firm helping compliance and ethics professionals to develop fantastic training and communications tools. Ricardo reached out to me when I started Spark Compliance Consulting to encourage me and to give me advice. I've never forgotten it. Here, Ricardo shares his thoughts on the future of training and communications.

Kristy: You've done some really creative things regarding compliance and ethics training. What is your favorite piece of work or innovation?

Ricardo: I think I'm most proud of our work on reframing the goal of compliance training from "knowledge" to "behavior." That's not a radical or novel concept, but it's largely been discussed piecemeal or as an abstraction. I think Broadcat was the first firm to articulate a practical framework – what we need to do in terms of content, delivery, and measurement so that compliance officers could actually put the framework into practice.

Of course, I'm happy when people like the visual appeal or simplicity of our work – because that's really hard to get right. But those things are ultimately tools that fit into this framework, not ends in themselves. So I really love it when someone tells us that we've totally changed how they think about the problem, because that's what we're going for.

Kristy: I've heard you talk extensively about the difference between sit-at-the-desk-for-an-hour standard training and effective training. Can you describe the difference?

Ricardo: Effective compliance training is focused on driving specific behaviors. Practically, that means it's framed around a specific behavior. The training must be delivered as close in time as possible to when the behavior occurs, and the outcomes need to be measured by business impact.

That all may sound pretty obvious, but it's the opposite of how most compliance training is done. While effective training focuses on behavior, standard training focuses on knowledge acquisition – which is the wrong goal and massively over-complicates things.

Here's a simple analogy: let's say your compliance mandate was reducing traffic fatalities at a certain intersection in your city. Standard training protocols would dictate a 30-minute module on why it's important to stop at that specific intersection. It would be issued to drivers on an annual basis via e-learning, and would be measured by quizzes that tested how well people memorized where the intersection was located and what they needed to do there.

Effective training, on the other hand, would mean putting up stop signs at the intersection. It'd be measured by whether traffic fatalities went down or not. It's honestly just a lot simpler.

Kristy: How do you see the future of training and communications in compliance?

Ricardo: My hope is that we see a major course correction in how we think about these things. Because we've historically viewed compliance training failures as a learning or memory problem, the "innovations" are basically just the same thing in a fancier format that we hope will boost learning and retention. That has made us way too focused on training fads and not nearly enough on what problem compliance training is really supposed to address: mitigating risk by changing specific behaviors.

So I'd like to see a future where we stop focusing on apps and skits and videos while still talking about risks at a high level (which is essentially celebrating training for the sake of training). Instead, I'd like to see us focus on using training as a tool to change specific behaviors.

I'd like to see people saying, "here's how we got our managers to catch red flags in third-party invoices," even though that's a little less sexy than "here's a snazzy video we made about ethics." That kind of incremental behavioral change is how we will actually advance and conquer as a profession.

Kristy: What's your best advice for compliance officers trying to make their program effective for employees?

Ricardo: Focus on solving problems for employees, not yourself. There are way too many compliance processes and systems that optimize things for compliance teams but not for employees. That's a path to having a program that is easy to run but doesn't actually help anyone.

For example, your average whistle-blower hotline makes it easy for the compliance team to process data but requires employees to input 100 different pieces of information before they're allowed to submit their concern. You can talk all you want about the importance of speaking up, but if the actual process of speaking up is a bureaucratic nightmare, then no one will do it.

If you think about your role as making it easy for employees to do their jobs compliantly and raise concerns when they have them, it will transform how you do specific initiatives like training and policies and hotline management – but it will also transform how you allocate your time.

You'll find that you spend less time on top-down, high-level initiatives like rebranding your Code of Conduct for the ten-thousandth time or having the perfect speaker for your compliance week event. Those things are fine to do, but they're too high-level to help any specific person do their job compliantly.

Instead, you'll start spending more and more time on bottom-up, employee-focused initiatives where you drill into specific processes and jobs and help them understand how to mitigate risk in their context.

And because compliance failures happen at the level of specific job duties – not at some level of abstraction – that type of specific, employee-focused work is how you'll ultimately be effective.

Chapter 12: Putting it All Together

"Nothing is impossible, the word itself says 'I'm possible'!"
– Audrey Hepburn

Congratulations! Your career in compliance is underway. You've decided to follow this path, updated your CV, chosen where you want to go, negotiated your way into a job, established your profile, and collaborated swimmingly with those around you. What happens next? You'll do it all over again. Such is the nature of the job – the continual reinvention and reinvestment of yourself in this incredible career.

Where Are You Going and How Will You Get There?

Think about where you'd like to be in one, five and ten years' time. Is it higher up in your current company? Is it going from corporate life into government or private practice? Perhaps you intend to take a short break for maternity/paternity, or to take care of an aging parent, then come back to your career. Complete the following with one or two sentences. You don't have to know exactly where you'll be. It may be better to avoid, "In five years, I'll be at XYZ Corporation as their Chief Compliance Officer," and instead say, "In five years, I'll be at a large regional or national company as Chief Compliance Officer."

a.   In one year, I'll be:

_____

_____

_____

b.   In five years, I'll be:

_____

_____

_____

c.   In ten years, I'll be:

_____

_____

_____

Think about what you can do now in order to build into the person who will be an obvious candidate for the job you'll want in one, five and ten years' time. Write down five concrete actions you can take to move you closer to your goals. These actions may include finding a mentor, writing articles, being on panel sessions at conferences, learning a new skill set, becoming certified, or anything you can think of that will make you more hirable as a candidate.

1.

_____

_____

2.

_____

_____

3.

_____

_____

4.

_____

_____

5.

_____

_____

Now say out loud, "I will complete all of these tasks to become a Wildly Successful compliance professional."

Put at least one of the activities you wrote above into your calendar. Add the activities to your task list, give them each a deadline and begin to work on them. Time passes quickly, and without committing to the tasks that will advance your career, it's all too easy to be in the same place year after year. Commit to yourself – you're worth it!

Commit to yourself – you're worth it!

Case Study: Joe Murphy's Top Ten Tips for Having a Wildly Successful Career in Compliance

Joe Murphy has been a leader in the field of compliance and ethics before we even knew it was a field. Here are his top ten tips for having a Wildly Successful career in compliance:

1. **Listen.** Listen actively and with all you can give it. Listening is not just politely waiting for the other person to stop so you can talk. Listening is a skill to learn and practice.

2. **Public speaking.** Study, learn, and practice it. It is a skill you have to study and develop.

3. **The Wall Street Journal.** Read it, every day. Know what is happening in the world and what is going to happen.

4. **Network.** Network with peers, with authors, and with speakers. Read their ideas, and share your experiences. Tell them what you liked.

5. **Partner.** Partner with someone you like and trust, and has complementary skills. My first two books were co-written with an accomplished author. My business success was partially due to the skills of a quietly brilliant leader.

6. **Respect.** Respect, but don't defer to leaders. Respect and listen to the workers and those in the field.

7. **Have two to five reasons**. When I do something, I usually have two to five reasons for doing so. If there is more

than one reason to do something, it will have more effect, and my time will be better utilized.

8. **Failures and mistakes.** I hate them! With a passion. However, I have learned my best lessons from failures and mistakes. After each one, buckle down and learn from it.

9. **Be in the field.** Executives think they know what's going on. The workers actually do. Spend time in the remote sales office, with a junior staff person in HQ and as the Australians say, at the coalface. Do a ride along; answer some customer calls. Live the business for a time.

10. **Speak up for compliance and ethics**. Champion our cause. Success is not only outward, but inward. Feel good about how you have promoted this field. Get involved in championing compliance and ethics.

Speak up for compliance and ethics. Champion our cause.

Finally, a word about success. Success is not only outward, but inward. There will be only so many Chief Ethics and Compliance Officers and well-known speakers and authors. But what is success? Suppose "all" you ever do is save one father from injury at work to go home to see his young daughter because a dangerous work condition you helped prevent didn't kill him. Suppose all you ever did is save one young lady's career because she did not do some incredibly stupid anti-competitive act. Suppose all you did is prevent a thousand babies from being deformed because you insisted on telling the truth to the FDA. Chances are, no one will ever know. But you will know. And what better success is there than knowing that you have made a real difference in people's lives.

From Me: What I Know for Sure

Compliance is an ever-changing world. Regulations change, CEOs (and the managers who go with them) change, and regulators' expectations change. But some things stay consistent. This is what I know for sure:

I'm sure soft skills like listening and communication will become ever more important for people wishing to grow into senior compliance roles.

I'm sure technology will continue to evolve, and with that evolution, new solutions will appear that will make our jobs more automated and easier. I'm sure we don't need to be afraid of that.

I'm sure regulation will continue to grow, and new laws, legal decisions and best practices will come into place, which will challenge all of us to evolve our compliance programs.

I'm sure that spending time building your network is one of, if not the most important things you can do to create opportunities and broaden your career prospects.

I'm sure that speaking and writing articles or blogs is the best way to cement your knowledge of a topic, and the fastest way to be seen as an expert in the field.

I'm sure that participating within the compliance community via conference attendance, blog commenting and LinkedIn will make you better known, and therefore more likely to be recommended or hired.

And I know, deep in my soul, that what we are doing in this profession is changing the world.

My Hope for a Better World

I hope that this book has inspired you to grow your career in compliance. I hope that this book has helped you to consider where your career might take you, and given you tools for growing yourself and your profile so you can make the most of your talents within the profession.

And I know, deep in my soul, that what we are doing in this profession is changing the world.

There will be setbacks. Some days will feel deeply lonely. You'll think you're the only person in the world who feels completely ostracized. Other days you'll be remarkably bored. You'll wonder if the work of pushing paper, checking boxes, and drafting another dull policy that nearly no one will read is worthwhile. "Is this all there is?" you'll wonder.

During the bad times, come back to your mission. As I've said in every book I've written, you are part of a movement that is changing how the world does business. Never forget that bribery was much more commonplace not so long ago – a totally accepted part of business. Never forget that not so long ago, banks didn't worry about money laundering, and didn't really need to know their customers. Never forget that not so long ago modern slavery was an under-the-rug issue that no one ever investigated within the supply chain of a company. We're making a difference – every day – in the lives of real people.

You are part of a critical movement. Most of all, I hope you realize how important you are in the quest to make the world a better place for everyone. Each of us within this profession is having a profound impact on the way organizations do business. Thank you for standing up to take your place amongst the compliance superheroes. I am honored to be part of your profession.

Acknowledgements

This book would not have been possible without the incredible collaboration of the compliance community. I am deeply grateful to everyone who answered my survey, provided comments, and gave their insight to make this book possible. I especially want to thank Lisa Beth Lentini, Sue Gainor, Hugh Bigwood, Rob Baron, Ricardo Pellafone, Tania Pavaskar, and the inimitable Joe Murphy for their additions.

Thank you to Erin Larison, my fearless editor, for continually making my writing better than it should be.

On a personal note, thank you to my incredibly loving family, including my fiercely powerful and remarkable sisters, Kelly Wood and Kimberly Black. To my mother, Kathy Elwood, to whom this book is dedicated – thank you for all of your love and unending support through the years. To my father, Kerry S. Grant, who continues as a deeply loving presence in my life, even from the other side. And to my stepparents, Linda Grant and Michael Elwood, who have loved me as their own.

Thank you to my dear friends – Marnie Smilen, Natalie Leon Walsh, Alison Charbonneau, Jenny Zdenak, Michele Moore Fried, Megan Tepper, Lisa Hall, Chris Van Etten, and Rachel Mendoza. Life wouldn't be half as fun without you!

Thank you also to my wonderful Sparkie family, especially my business partner, Diana Trevley. You are a great gift.

Lastly, to my deeply adored husband, Jonathan Grant-Hart. You continue to be my greatest gift, my fondest friend, and the love of my life. My gratitude and love for you knows no end.

About the Author

Kristy Grant-Hart is an expert in designing and implementing effective compliance programs for multi-national companies. She is a professional speaker, author, former professor, and thought leader in the compliance profession. She is the founder and CEO of Spark Compliance Consulting, an international consulting company focusing on pragmatic and pro-business anti-bribery, anti-slavery, ISO 37001 and data privacy solutions.

Ms. Grant-Hart formerly served as Chief Compliance Officer for United International Pictures, the joint distribution company for Paramount Pictures and Universal Pictures in 65+ countries. While there, she was shortlisted for the Chief Compliance Officer of the Year award at the Women in Compliance Awards.

Ms. Grant-Hart was an Adjunct Professor at Delaware School of Law, Widener University teaching Global Compliance and Ethics. Ms. Grant-Hart began her legal career at the international law firm of Gibson, Dunn & Crutcher, where she worked in the firm's Los Angeles and London offices.

She lives in London with her husband and beloved rescue dogs, Samuel and Mr. Fox.

Index

Notes

[1] Linda Babcock & Sarah Laschever, Ask for It: How Women Can Use the Power of Negotiation to Get What They Really Want, Location 1015 Kindle edition (Bantam Dell 2008)

[2] Sheryl Sandberg, Lean In: Women, Work and the Will to Lead 101 (Alfred A. Knopf 2013)

[3] Nancy F. Clark, Act Now To Shrink The Confidence Gap, Forbes (April 28, 2014), https://www.forbes.com/sites/womensmedia/2014/04/28/act-now-to-shrink-the-confidence-gap/#23d323f65c41

[4] Lois P. Frankel, Nice Girls Don't Get the Corner Office: Unconscious Mistakes Women Make That Sabotage Their Careers 24 (Hatchet Book Group 2004)

[5] Napoleon Hill, The Law of Success: The Master Wealth-Builder's Complete and Original Lesson Plan for Achieving Your Dreams, Location 65 Kindle edition (Jeremy P. Tarcher 1928)

[6] Carmine Gallo, Talk Like TED: the 9 Public Speaking Secrets of the World's Top Minds 135 (MacMillan 2014)

[7] Megyn Kelly, How Megyn Kelly Deals With Online Bullies, O, The Oprah Magazine (Hearst Publications 2016) http://www.oprah.com/inspiration/megyn-kelly-online-bullying

[8] Jack Canfield, The Success Principles, Location 3055 Kindle edition (HarperCollins e-books 2014)

www.ingramcontent.com/pod-product-compliance
Lightning Source LLC
Chambersburg PA
CBHW060305220326
41598CB00027B/4244